A CITIZEN'S GUIDE TO AMERICAN IDEOLOGY

Conservatives and Liberals often resort to cartoon images of the opposing ideology, relying on broadly defined caricatures to illustrate their opposition. To help us get past these stereotypes, this short, punchy book explains the two dominant political ideologies in America today, providing a thorough and fair analysis of each as well as insight into their respective branches.

To help us understand the differences between the two contrasting ideologies, Morgan Marietta employs an innovative metaphor of a tree—growth from ideological roots to a core value, expanding into a problem that creates the competing branches of the ideology. This approach suggests a clear way to explain and compare the two ideologies in an effort to enhance democratic debate.

A Citizen's Guide to American Ideology is a brief, non-technical, and conversational overview of one of the most important means of understanding political rhetoric and policy debates in America today.

Morgan Marietta is Visiting Assistant Professor in the Department of Political Science at the University of Georgia.

CITIZEN GUIDES TO POLITICS AND PUBLIC AFFAIRS

Morgan Marietta and Bert Rockman, Series Editors

Each book in this series is framed around a significant but not well-understood subject that is integral to citizens'—both students and the general public—full understanding of politics and participation in public affairs. In accessible language, these titles provide readers with the tools for understanding the root issues in political life. Individual volumes are brief and engaging, written in short, readable chapters without extensive citations or footnoting. Together they are part of an essential library to equip us all for fuller engagement with the issues of our times.

TITLES IN THE SERIES

A CITIZEN'S GUIDE TO AMERICAN IDEOLOGY

Conservatism and Liberalism in Contemporary Politics

Morgan Marietta

Routledge
Taylor & Francis Group
NEW YORK AND LONDON

First published 2012
by Routledge
711 Third Avenue, New York, NY 10017

Simultaneously published in the UK
by Routledge
2 Park Square, Milton Park, Abingdon, Oxon OX14 4RN

Routledge is an imprint of the Taylor & Francis Group, an informa business

Library of Congress Cataloging in Publication Data
A citizen's guide to American ideology:
conservatism and liberalism in contemporary politics /
Morgan Marietta.
p. cm.
Includes bibliographical references and index.
1. Conservatism–United States. 2. Liberalism–United States.
Ideology–United States. I. Title.
JC573.2.U6M349 2011
320.50973–dc23
20110109602

ISBN: 978–0–415–89899–7 (hbk)
ISBN: 978–0–415–89900–0 (pbk)
ISBN: 978–0–203–18309–0 (ebk)

Typeset in Garamond
by Swales & Willis Ltd, Exeter, Devon

FOR MY STUDENTS

CONTENTS

ILLUSTRATIONS

Figures

Tables

ACKNOWLEDGMENTS

This book originated in lectures given to my students at Colgate University, Bates College, Hamilton College, and the University of Georgia, and more importantly in the discussions that followed with many sharp minds testing their own perspectives on American politics. The book is dedicated to students of our national conversation, in and beyond university classes.

Many thanks are due to Michael Kerns at Routledge Press, who supported this series and its goal of speaking to a broad audience about essential political questions. My friend and colleague Bert Rockman was also instrumental in making the series possible.

Several students deserved special thanks for their comments on early drafts of the manuscript, including Will Burgess, Wells Ellenberg, Addie Hampton, and John Shapiro. I would also like to thank David Barker, Jeff Condran, Sam DeCanio, Robert Holzbach, Glenn Kent, Meredith Leland, and Robert Peluso, as well as Abby Williams and the rest of the clan, including Alix, Dan, Justin, David, and Ken. As always, I am indebted to Mark Perlman who inspired my desire to understand the nature of belief, and watched it grow at his table. *Noscitur e sociis*—if a man is known by his associates, I wish no better company.

INTRODUCTION
Too Common and Too Rare

If you ask many liberals what conservatives are, they will say "mean people." Liberals are nice people who want to help others, and conservatives are selfish and uncaring. From the other perspective, many conservatives define liberalism as simply being foolish. Liberals are idealistic souls who have no clear grasp of the harsher realities of the world, both domestic and foreign. A line I've heard many times is that if you are a conservative while young, you have no heart, but if you are still a liberal by the time you are old, you have no brain. If one bought into these views, it would present a difficult choice: would you rather be mean or foolish? Hard to say. Better to understand the two worldviews accurately so we can embrace or reject them for what they truly are rather than resort to cartoon images.

The purpose of this brief book is to explain American ideology. What is conservatism and what is liberalism? This is not meant to be an intellectual history of the two movements, or an academic account of the various strains of ideological thought over time and in different nations, but instead simply a discussion of citizen politics in contemporary America. The goal is to describe what it means to be conservative or liberal in the present day from the perspective of a politically interested citizen. When we identify what it means to hold an ideology in our current politics, it becomes clear that most Americans do not have one. They are not fully fledged liberals or conservatives, and do not offer these complete worldviews with their ready-made responses to current events. Often an individual citizen's values lean to the conservative side or tend to be more liberal, but this is very different from holding a full political ideology.

From the perspective of many citizens, ideology is far too common. Our political elites and media personalities discuss ideology (and are driven by it) routinely. We hear the rhetoric of liberalism versus conservatism in regard to almost any issue, when discussed by almost any commentator. Many of our citizens would prefer a less ideological politics. They often react negatively to the ideologies of our public debates because their own beliefs are not ideological. But from the perspective of our political elites, whether in government, media, or academics, ideology is far too rare. Many believe that being non-ideological is the same as being uninformed or even irresponsible. They see their ideology as natural and virtuous, and look down on non-ideologues, or in other words, most citizens. Those citizens often see ideologues as odd or extreme and do not trust them. It is normal and unremarkable for Americans to hold values or opinions that are conservative in some senses and liberal in others, but to our leadership class this seems strange and wrong-headed. One of the important observations about ideology in America is that our political elites have it in spades, while most of our citizens are not guided by the same ideas that motivate our leaders. From these different perspectives, ideology is seen as either too far common or far too rare. This creates serious problems for communication between citizens and politicians, and makes it difficult for the public to keep track of what our leaders are up to.

So what are the liberal or conservative ideologies that drive our political elites? The first thing to note is that it is not a single dimension, which is how American ideology is usually discussed. There is no meaningful left–right continuum because conservatism and liberalism are not opposites. Instead they are two distinct worldviews that emphasize different assumptions about how the world works, different core values, and very different visions of a good society. This is the heart of a political ideology: a constellation of values and assumptions that organize a comprehensive view of how to improve our society. These assumptions and values and future visions are not really opposites. The competing worldviews create different core questions about how we ought to act. Conservatism and liberalism are not different answers to the same question, but pose different questions altogether. It is not the case that the central question of conservatism is answered differently by liberals. Instead, liberals do even see it as a meaningful question. The same is true in the reverse. Liberalism poses a question that is of little concern to conservatives. Each worldview does not understand the other a great deal of the time, which explains why liberals and conservatives often talk past each other without engaging in the same conversation. It also explains why members of each group have trouble describing their opponents accurately. Most true ideologues cannot express what the other camp believes without employing terms of insult, except by assuming it is the opposite of their beliefs, which is not at all accurate.

2

A second crucial note about ideology is that conservatism is not one thing, but has several distinct branches that sometimes conflict with each other. Liberalism is also internally divided. This might sound as if the two ideologies are the same in this sense, both being divided into competing factions, but again the real situation is not as it is often described. Conservatism is divided into branches that reflect different answers to the core question of the ideology, but they often overlap and can be compatible as well as competitive. Liberalism is divided in a different way that is often a zero-sum form of competition. The different answers to the core question of liberalism are competitive rather than cooperative, creating a deeper form of division within that ideology.

The following chapters summarize the conservative and liberal worldviews, and then compare the two ideologies. The book makes three central points. The most important is that conservatism and liberalism do not form a single dimension or continuum. Instead they are distinct worldviews grounded in competing core values and premises about reality, which lead to different questions and proposed answers for our society. Conservative concerns focus on the Glue Problem, or how to maintain a free and decent society given the forces of threat and decline, while liberalism focuses on the Oppression Problem, or which group in society deserves our attention and support in order to achieve equality. Conservatism centers on *protecting* society, while liberalism focuses on *perfecting* society.

The second point is that each ideology has competing branches. The answers to the two worldviews' core questions divide the ideologies into different types of conservatives and types of liberals, depending on how they believe the glue problem should be answered, or which social group is most oppressed and deserving of support. However, the branches are more cooperative on the conservative side and competitive among liberals.

The final point is that full-blown ideologies are the province of political elites, compared to the less complex political values of ordinary citizens. This creates a meaningful distance between electoral politics and public policy decisions. It distorts the nature of representation in our political system, and limits the communication between elites and normal citizens.

While ideology is pervasive in our political conversation, it is rarely understood even by the political elites who hold one worldview but cannot explain the other. The following chapters attempt to clarify these competing ideologies, written for citizens who are either one, or neither one, but wish to understand both.

1

AN IDEOLOGY TREE

Sometimes it is best to begin defining something by what it isn't. This is especially true if a common misconception muddies the waters. From the time Americans began to conduct surveys on public opinion, attitudes about policy proposals have been the central focus. The idea was that democracy is about following the will of the people, so the key is knowing what citizens think about each proposed policy change. There is always a left and a right side, and people who are consistently on the right are conservatives, and the ones who line up on the left are liberals. Citizens have political stances, and ideology is a simple matter of which side of the policy debates they are on. The problem is that *both of these assumptions are wrong*. Most citizens do not have stable policy opinions about most issues. They are concerned more about their daily lives than following policy debates, so most have not really thought about and decided where they stand on the majority of issues. The second assumption—that ideology is the combination of these policy preferences—is also false, because issue positions do not lead to ideology, but the reverse. Ideology is what makes people hold consistent issue positions. Policy preferences don't cause ideology; ideology causes policy preferences.

Fifty years ago a professor named Phil Converse wrote a paper that changed how we understand American ideology. The mythology about the paper is that it went around to the major academic journals, all of which refused to publish it because the reviewers thought it couldn't possibly be right. It eventually appeared as a famous chapter in a relatively obscure book. Converse looked at the evidence from the public opinion surveys that had been growing in number over the previous decade, and realized that most citizens did not have consistent opinions from one year to the next. When asked about current issues, they would not admit ignorance, but just make something up. Perhaps even more important was his discovery that, along with lacking policy views, most citizens did not have an identifiable ideology. Only 10 to 15 percent of Americans were in any way ideological, and most of the rest had trouble explaining what conservatism and liberalism were.[1]

The reason this paper was almost never published is that it reflects a reality exactly the opposite of the assumptions of most people in government and the academic world. From the perspective of ideological people who took politics seriously in their daily lives, it was unthinkable that other Americans did not follow politics, or have ready policy opinions, and fulfill their role in the academic understanding of democratic theory. But all of the collective evidence since that time indicates that Converse was correct, then and still today.

The lack of a constraining ideology in large part explains the lack of stable policy preferences, as those are often the *result* of an ideology rather than a building block of one. Few people work out in detail their policy positions on a broad range of issues, which would take a tremendous amount of reading and effort. Even if they did, this process would be unlikely to result in positions that were all conservative or all liberal. It is the reverse process—determining an ideology first—that results in liberal or conservative positions across the board, once the ideology gives us a shortcut to how we should see individual issues. It is the ideology that controls the policy views, rather than the opposite. Once we see that most Americans do not have a hardcore ideology, it follows that they would tend to not have hardline policy views either.

Academics who study public opinion have accepted that most citizens and voters are not ideological, but they have not gotten over their disappointment. For professionals in polling, this led to a dilemma that still plagues the entire industry of public opinion studies: if democracy is about following the policy choices of the majority, how can it work if citizens do not have informed policy preferences? A good question, which is still at the heart of arguments over American democracy among academics.[2] We can't solve that problem here, but one possible answer is that democracy is not about policy preferences after all. In other words, we started by looking for the wrong thing. Democracy is about the core values of citizens, and making sure that our leaders share those values. The central question is the shifting balance in our competing value divisions:

- Do we believe that individuals are responsible for themselves or that society is responsible for the welfare of all of our citizens?
- Do we believe in a more secular or religious public culture?
- Do we accept that military force is a necessary feature of international affairs or believe that we should employ force only as an absolute last resort?

5

- Should we shun involvement in the affairs of other nations or accept the responsibilities of a superpower to improve conditions overseas and advance our values?
- Should we make a commitment to the environment and the survival of other species as an end in itself or give priority to other interests and commitments?
- Should we embrace traditional roles between men and women, husbands and wives, parents and children, or be open to new understandings and social arrangements?

These questions of core value commitments are at the heart of our politics. In order to see their role in American ideology, we have to discuss the different forms of belief that citizens hold. One description that may be both simple and accurate is an ideology tree.

An Ideology Tree

The right metaphor may be the key to explaining something. It is the best image that matches the topic. For example, ideology resembles a tree. It has

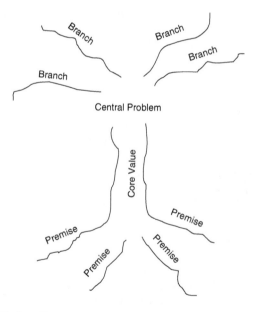

Figure 1.1 An Ideology Tree

roots, or foundations, that lead to a trunk, or the main argument. Those create a central question or problem that limits the height of the tree. At that point there are different answers, which lead to the branches or competing factions within the ideology. Conservatism and liberalism are both like this, but have different foundations and distinct core values, which lead to different central questions and then competing answers, or the branches of the ideology.

An ideology tree grows from different kinds of beliefs that create a unified worldview. The two key forms of belief that define an ideology are *values* and *premises*. The first are statements about how the world *should* work; the second are observations about how the world *does* work. Statements of desirable principle and immutable practice—of goals and realities—these are the roots of ideology.

Values

Values are difficult to define, but we can begin with the observation that *values need no justification, but we can justify nothing without them*. All of our political judgments of right or wrong, better or worse, rely on values. They are "not means to ends, but ultimate ends, ends in themselves."[3] Among the competing priorities for a good society, values are standing judgments of which ones are better. For example, do we believe that tradition is good and a source of stability, or do we embrace new social arrangements that challenge the old status quo, like gay marriage? This is not the same question as what we would ban or enforce, but what in our hearts do we feel is *better*? Should we publicly respect military people and their service, or should we wish for a different world that does not require military force and shift admiration to nonviolent protestors? Again the question is less about specific policies and more about what we admire.

Another way of thinking of values is that they are the *backstops* of our decisions. If we ask someone to explain a political position, and then press them to justify that reason, and continue in this fashion, the point at which they can go no further is a value. At some point we arrive at a statement that it feels silly to justify. We reach the baseline position that human life is good, or that you desire individual freedom, or that more equality is better. These are the things that seem obvious to you, needing no justification. They are simply true. They are the core of our belief system, and we are attached to them at a gut level. Hence, values—the most reduced form of justification—can only be believed rather than justified.

In addition to being backstops, values can be thought of as *meta-prefer-ences*. 'Meta' as a prefix makes a word apply to itself, or in this case, prefer-ences about preferences. A simple choice or preference for something is not a value, but a preference about other peoples' choices is. For example, you might prefer dogs to cats (being a reasonable person). That is a simple preference, but not a political value. If you would prefer that *other people* prefer dogs, which would be to want a more doggish and less cattish world, that would be a value. Many reasonable people prefer dogs, but have no concern about the expansion of cat lovers; their love of dogs, while noble, is a simple preference. When we move from the realm of personal preferences to public desires, those are values. This explains why a com-mon rejoinder to citizens who oppose legal abortion—that they simply shouldn't have one—is missing the point. Values are not merely personal choices, but hopes for what is normal or acceptable, public rather than private preferences.

Premises

We began with values, but in some ways it is *premises* that are the real foun-dations of an ideological worldview. What is the world really like? More importantly, what are *people* really like? Basic assumptions about these ques-tions determine perhaps more than anything else how we will see politics. These assumptions are so basic that they seem to defy needing evidence; they are obvious. It may be more accurate to say that they can't be demon-strated with the available evidence, one way or the other. We simply don't know the true answers to some of the most important questions. So we disagree strongly, though most people trust their own feelings.

Some of the most influential premises are about human nature. Are peo-ple naturally good? Born with innate tendencies to be bad? Aggressive and violent, or by nature peaceful and only driven to violence when pushed? Rational or driven by irrational impulses? Are they simply what they are, or can they change? Does human nature even exist, or are people more mal-leable than that? The answers to these questions can be thought of as natural truths, or the simple conditions of human reality. But they are not fully sepa-rate from values. We can think of statements about *what ought to be* and state-ments about *what is* as fundamentally distinct, but they are intertwined in unavoidable ways. For example, we may believe that military service ought to be publicly admired and highly respected. This is distinct from the belief that the world is a dangerous place and filled with implacable enemies. The first is a value and the second a premise, but they are strongly connected in

8

our belief systems. Premises are not merely facts, but value-laden facts, or idealized facts. Values and premises are intertwined in ways that reinforce each other.

Why individuals hold specific premises is not clear. Perhaps they heard them repeatedly as a child, from parents and other influences. Perhaps they picked up certain premises from the surrounding culture, or from personal experiences that ingrained a perspective on other people. A specific religious tradition could have communicated a premise through its stories and sermons. Hard to say. We don't know exactly how premises originate, but we do know that people have very different perceptions of how the world works and what people are like—what the real facts of reality are.

Ideology

With the building blocks of premises and values in mind, we can identify a clear definition of an ideology: *a specific constellation of connected values and premises that create a vision of a good society.* With that guiding vision, the ideology identifies the social changes or government actions that would lead to that better world. A set of policy preferences flows naturally from an ideology, something that has been described as "the conversion of ideas into social levers."[4]

A specific grouping of premises and values leading to a political agenda may be the clearest definition, but an ideology is also something broader, what could be called a worldview. It is a way to understand yourself and your position in society, a way to make sense of your story. It is most powerful at its most personal, tying emotions to individual experiences to social possibilities. Ideology can take impersonal events and give them personal meaning. If it doesn't connect to a sense of your own history, it is likely to mean very little. The famous anthropologist Clifford Geertz wrote that "ideologies transform sentiment into significance."[5] They change incomprehensible realities into understandable beliefs.

Table 1.1 summarizes the forms of belief we have identified, or the nature of values, premises, and ideologies. But the most important illustration in this chapter is clearly the ideology tree. It illustrates how our most basic political concepts of premises and values create the cohesive worldview of an ideology. The following chapters explain the four distinct parts of conservative and liberal ideology: the foundational premises, the core values, the central questions, and their competitive answers that divide each ideology into different branches.

Table 1.1 Forms of Belief

Value	A standing judgment of competing social ends or priorities. A meta-preference (a public rather than private value). A backstop for decision-making.
Premise	A belief or assumption about empirical reality. A standing judgment of how people are.
Ideology	A specific constellation of values and premises that lead to a vision of a good society or plan for social action, including specific policy proposals.

Part I

CONSERVATISM

2

CONSERVATISM

Premise Foundations

The three premises of conservatism can be thought of as separate foundations that lead to a conservative worldview. They also combine to form a
cohesive whole. To accept one of them would lead you toward conservatism; to believe all three virtually guarantees it.

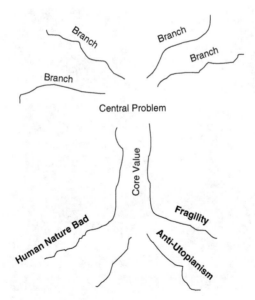

Figure 2.1 Conservative Premises

Fragility

"Are there barbarians at the gate?" The conservative answer to this question is "Yes." We do have enemies, and they are often at the gates. Perhaps the most basic conservative premise is the fragility of a democratic society.

The question evokes several different images. What it means to different people can illustrate something significant about their premises. One possible image is external enemies attacking us, literal barbarians like those at the Gates of Rome. In the contemporary world, these enemies were fascists in World War II, international communists during the Cold War, and now terrorists. How likely are attacks, and how able are we to withstand them?

Another image is internal enemies corrupting us. These include criminals, drug addicts, child-abusers, or simply irresponsible people who cannot take care of themselves and neglect their children, who then end up being criminals, drug addicts, or child-abusers, repeating the cycle. In addition to external enemies and internal miscreants, the phrase also refers to metaphorical barbarians, or simply Philistines who do not have decent values, self-restraint, or respect for good things. They are modern barbarians,

Figure 2.2 Genseric Sacking Rome by Karl Briullov

14

conquering the culture more with degraded behavior than with bat-tleaxes. *Jersey Shore* is not as much of a threat as a jihadi camp, but it is not good.

The question of barbarians at the gate really means, "Do we have things to fear?" If we have no real enemies, then this is not a concern. But if we do, then our national strength against foreign enemies and our moral strength against internal ones is a vital issue. The question is whether these enemies are a real threat. Opinions differ widely, based not just on their strength, but on our fragility. In the 2008 Democratic Presidential Debates, among the eight candidates on the stage in the initial rounds was Mike Gravel, the former Senator from Alaska, noted for releasing the Pentagon Papers during the Vietnam War. When asked who our most important enemies were, he responded, "We have no important enemies. . . . Who are we afraid of? I'm not." To Gravel, there are no wolves at the door. To a conservative, his statement is jarring to say the least. The political theorist Carl Schmitt called such sentiments the "illusions with which men like to deceive themselves regarding political realities in periods of untroubled security."[1] Schmitt famously argued that the basic political distinction is between friends and enemies; the weakness of democratic societies is that they often refuse to admit they have enemies. But the heart of the question is our own stability weighed against the strength of such threats, both external and internal. The Oath of Office taken by all members of the president's cabinet, members of the armed forces, and public officials, is to "support and defend the Constitution of the United States against all enemies, foreign and domestic." This is an under-appreciated piece of our political theory, which states clearly that we expect that our constitutional order—the basic ideas of a democracy—will have enemies, and not just among foreigners.

There are two parts of the fragility premise: that all human society is fragile, and that our society in particular is even more so. The first part assumes that things degenerate over time. The scientific term is *entropy*, or the observable law that the world tends toward disorder. Lacking an active force keeping them together, things fall apart. In addition to external violence and internal decay, it could result from human error, natural disaster, or economic depression, but mostly from just moral indecency and a decline in the willingness to sacrifice for the group.

The second part of the premise is the fragility in *our* system, or the inherent vulnerability of democratic societies. The conservative worldview sees the achievements of the Founding as the remarkable efforts of unique men, who forged radical concepts of individual freedom and limited government into a workable system. But that achievement was always known to be an experiment. It was a fragile thing that most of the Founders did not believe would last many generations. As Franklin said when asked what kind of government we had, "a Republic, if you can keep it." Our grand experiment in self-government was unheard of at that time and is still unusual in the world today. Most of the inhabitants of the world still live under one form of authoritarian rule or another and have no experience with a rights-based democracy. A decent world of protected rights and representative government is a rare thing beset by challengers. All societies and civilizations, even the strongest—even the Roman Empire—fall eventually. The Founders drew inspiration from two historical examples of democracy: the Greek city-states of antiquity and the Italian city-states of the Renaissance. Both groups succumbed to internal division and external enemies. The only questions are how much time we have, and how can we lengthen it.

The fragility premise may be the easiest way to understand a conservative worldview and conservative issue positions. If our society and the achievements of the Founding are fragile, then we need a strong military, a unified culture, the protection of God, and individual gun ownership, or, in short, all of the conservative political goals. The reverse is true if our democracy and society are essentially stable: we do not need to emphasize military power, can encourage multiple cultures, and do not need the stability or protection offered by religion, the respect for traditional family arrangements, or personal weapons. In the economic realm, the fragility premise leads to the emphasis on individual production and economic efficiency; if things are unstable, individuals need to compete over available resources, and our society needs to maximize the total economic output for national strength. If we do not need to worry about stability, then we can be concerned about fairness and equality rather than competition and efficiency. The issue positions of conservative and liberal ideologies will be discussed more fully in Chapter 13, but as a preview, the fragility premise does a great deal of the work in focusing conservative thinking.

Human Nature

Another central conservative premise is the basic nature of humans. The first part of the premise is that human nature clearly exists. We are what we are, and that thing is not changing. As for the second part, what we are is not necessarily good. We are born selfish and aggressive. We might *become* good, but that is through positive examples, training, and restraint, not by accident or nature.

16

One way to think of this premise is to consider what you make of babies and small children. In your experience, are they selfless, good-natured, and giving, or self-seeking, prone to lash out, and greedy? Will kids share their toys willingly or do they have to be taught to share? What do kids do on school playgrounds anywhere in America: they pick on the weak ones, bully the ones who are different, and create in-groups among the boys, and even more vicious cliques among the girls. Why will they always do this? Because they haven't been civilized yet, and some never make it there.

This can be summarized as an innately negative human nature, but by negative, we mean self-seeking, combative, and potentially aggressive. The shorthand is that human nature is bad, but this doesn't mean that all people are bad, just that all are prone to negative motivations. Some, however, are just bad. There will always be violent, vicious people. Crime and criminals are just a fact of life, not an aberration that can be fixed.[2] There will always be aggressive people who exploit others, as well as political leaders who attempt to dominate people when given the chance.

One way to determine your own premise about human nature is to consider *Lord of the Flies*. Many high schools still assign this classic novel by William Golding, and there is a good film version made in 1990. It tells the story of a group of boys stranded on an island. One of the decent older boys attempts to maintain order, but the more aggressive ones quickly take over and the story devolves into tribalism and violence. They come to believe there is a monster on the island, and sacrifice a pig's head on a spear—the Lord of the Flies—to appease him, before turning on the weakest members of the group. A classic question in literature classes is, "Who was the monster on the island?" Answer: *They* were. The question for us is whether the story sounds plausible or fanciful. Is that what people are or not? Conservatives tend to see *Lord of the Flies* as an accurate metaphor for a human society without civilized constraints.

It may be important to note that different premises are tied to distinct intellectual and religious traditions. One of the central ones regarding human nature is the battle between Rousseau and Hobbes in the history of Western philosophy. Jean-Jacques Rousseau believed that humans were born good, and only became corrupt through mistreatment and negative circumstances. Thomas Hobbes saw it differently, and his book *Leviathan* depicts a world much like Golding's island when we lack strong leaders to maintain order. Life in the state of nature, he famously said, is "nasty, brutish, and short" (which might also describe the negative view of children).[3]

Religious doctrine is also an important source of individual premises about human nature. Original sin and the free will doctrine are basic sources of a

17

negative view of man's nature and predicament. Both Catholic and Evangelical Protestant traditions see man as essentially corrupt. This is not true of some mainline Protestant denominations, which have a more positive view of humans (for example, Methodism). The more a person absorbed the Evangelical or Catholic worldview while growing up, the more likely they are to hold negative premises about human nature. *Corrupt* may be the best word to describe these religions traditions: the human heart may not be bad, but it is corruptible. One of my favorite lines from *The Simpsons* is Homer's description of how his wife Marge has manipulated him: "She knows my weakness—it's that I'm weak!" The question is how well does that observation characterize most humans?

The Anti-Utopian Impulse

A different way to understand conservatism is through its anti-utopian premise, or a fundamental rejection of the utopian dream. Because of what humans are (often bad), and what societies are (always fragile), we have no real hope of a perfect world. Utopian visions that believe people can become better and societies can reach a state of harmonious grace are simple fantasies. Whether Marxist or Maoist, religious or secular, a technological metropolis or an agrarian commune, they are all false. And not merely wrong, but lead directly to more misery. The utopian impulse always leads to oppression and violence, because dissent will rise and dissent must then be destroyed in order to maintain unity and control. This occurs in all utopian movements, as the group orientation destroys individual dignity, either slowly or quickly.

In *Dr. Zhivago*—a classic story of utopian movements destroying a good man and his homeland—one of the revolutionary leaders says, "People will be different after the Revolution." This is one of the basic ideas of utopian thought: that human nature can change. Of course this is the exact opposite of the conservative premise about humans. This does not mean that things cannot become better. Incremental improvements in our institutions and conditions are possible, but *we* are the same, and attempts at improving society will fail if they do not recognize this reality. This explains the conservative suspicion of government programs that rely on goodwill and appreciation rather than incentives and markets. Incremental improvement can be positive, but most government actions are not in this category. Instead they are harmful because they do not have their intended effects. The *law of unintended consequences* plagues all attempts at social engineering. When we try to change the social order, we can influence things, but usually in a way we didn't anticipate. The best we can do is keep the trolls under their bridges where they belong. This is what good and valiant men do. But we should not delude ourselves into thinking that we can rid ourselves of trolls, because they breed too fast for that.

We can see now how the three premises of social fragility, negative human nature, and utopian failure are linked. Each reinforces the others as well as being important in its own right. Perhaps all three are summarized in a line by Sir John Barry, a former Justice of the Supreme Court of Victoria, Australia. He wrote in a letter to a friend who was an American professor, "One of the most dangerous things about your countrymen is the grim determination with which they cling to the belief in Santa Claus."[4] Conservatives attempt to grow out of childish beliefs about human nature, social stability, and the ability to perfect society through direct intervention. The broader question is the influence of these perceptions on the rest of conservatism, as the ideology grows from its foundations to its core value.

3

THE CORE VALUE OF CONSERVATISM

Ordered Liberty

The conservative premises center on fears: of instability, disorder, violence, and degradation, brought on by aggressive humans and foolish governments. These are powerful motivators grounded in what is feared. But what is desired?

The best phrase for the conservative core value is *ordered liberty*. This means freedom with decency, or liberty without license. The core value would simply be liberty if it were not for the premises discussed in the last

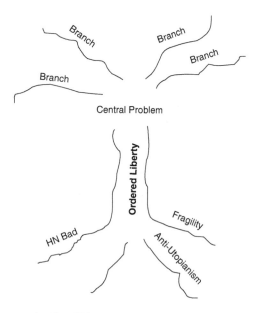

Figure 3.1 Conservative Core Value

chapter, which is why they are so central to the conservative worldview. If humans were naturally good and society were not fragile, liberty in and of itself would be the core value. However, the situation is more complex if we want liberty but know that people are problematic. We want a decent world, not merely a free one, a world in which we can raise children and have a sense of security for our families. Because people tend toward degradation, free societies trend toward decline, and utopian ideas are distracting fantasies, we must have ordered liberty, or the proper balance between individual freedoms and personal responsibilities .

It may sound contradictory to discuss liberty and its limits in the same breath, but the pioneers of a free society saw it exactly this way. The Founders of our constitutional order believed that rights and responsibilities were inseparable. That is what made the system work. Individuals were free to live their own lives, but were also expected to act decently and contribute to the defense of the system. The primary responsibility of able-bodied males was to defend society against threats, which is why all were members of the militia, or the inactive military body that organized when things went south. The Founding vision of intertwined liberties and responsibilities has been mostly abandoned in the contemporary world, but the resonance of that idea remains in conservative thought.

Ordered liberty means being a free person, with a free soul. It means being free from government telling us where to live, or what to think. Free from society making us worship in a certain way, or pay to support a church that is not ours. Churches, like homes, are private and never public things. It means being free from kings or nobles, people with titles who are by definition better than we are. This does not mean that distinctions in accomplishment, status, or wealth will not be important. They will be sought after and respected, even more so the more they are known to be due to fair competition rather than privilege or inheritance. But ordered liberty does not mean freedom just for the most powerful or aggressive, who can then control others. Freedom for all means that individuals must observe limits. We cannot steal, cannot use violence or intimidation, and should not be a burden to others nor exclude others from fair competition. We should not degrade the same society that supports us. This is the ethic of self-imposed restraint that is a central part of a conservative vision of a good society.

The distinction between *free* and *unfree* does not imply that there is no distinction between *appropriate* and *inappropriate*. Free and irresponsible are not synonymous. This is the case because liberty is not merely an end in itself. Liberty has a purpose, which is human dignity. Freedom for its own sake is not necessarily valuable and often leads to results that are exactly the opposite. Liberty has a different cast if we see it as having a higher purpose. This means not just a free but also a decent life, which includes security, decorum, civilized norms, respect for the worth of individuals, and regard for human excellence. Another way to phrase this is just because you *can* do something, does not mean you *should* do it, and we should not respect those who go too far. Decent restraint is just as much a part of a free society as liberty.

Ordered liberty is perhaps best defined as *balance*. Often there are two evils that we want to avoid, and veering too far to either side is our downfall. This kind of thinking can be described as seeking a *golden mean*, an idea we took from Greek philosophy. The intuition is that vices are found at the extremes and virtue in the middle. Any virtue taken to the extreme becomes a vice. This is true even of our greatest virtues, like love or charity, or even minor ones like caution. If we love someone else too much, we become fawning, obsessive, and ignore other people. It is unhealthy and leads to a bad end. If we take charity too far, we give away everything and leave nothing for ourselves, becoming paupers who can then give nothing. Caution is an important virtue, especially to conservatives, but too much leads to never leaving your house, or to an inability to take appropriate risks. In politics, the vices of the extremes are more clear: being too aggressive toward other nations versus being too weak and inviting attack; having too few police versus too many; having too little concern for the poor versus creating incentives for people to not work. The tension that may matter most in a democratic society is the choice between too little freedom and too much: the twin evils of tyranny and anarchy, the king and the mob. This is illustrated by the excesses of the French Revolution, which was inspired by our Revolution but then degraded into mob violence. Too little liberty and the King is putting people in prison; too much license and the mob is cutting off people's heads. The best path is the middle ground. This may be true of everything, but is the heart of a conservative view of politics. A free government must avoid the two opposing extremes of tyranny and disorder.

To be clear, a conservative golden mean is not at all the same as a moderate position. Intentional moderation suggests gauging where other citizens are and going down the middle. It is nothing more than following the herd by trying to not annoy its angriest members. Conservatism is deciding where we are in the balance between competing social evils, which may mean sometimes agreeing with the majority of our society and at other times opposing it. The balance of current opinion has nothing to do with the appropriate balance.

A few examples of golden mean thinking in the pursuit of ordered liberty explain a great deal about conservatism. In regard to *law enforcement*, conservatives tend to favor a strong police presence and harsh criminal penalties. This may sound like a contradiction. How can those in favor of liberty be in favor of locking people up, or even more striking, be in favor of state executions? Because citizens are free as well as responsible to others to not harm them with that freedom. If they do, it is not something to look lightly upon, because it robs other people of *their* freedom.

In some ways the law enforcement debate revolves around a disagreement about the purpose of the criminal justice system. There are four major theories: *punishment, deterrence, removal,* and *rehabilitation.* Punishment simply means that the belief in an eye for an eye offers an innate justice that is worth pursuing in its own right. Deterrence suggests that the larger purpose is to prevent rather than punish crime, while removal means that the real purpose is to keep dangerous people away from the rest of us. This is the idea behind three strikes laws that identify career criminals for permanent separation rather than limiting their punishment to each individual crime. Rehabilitation takes an entirely different view, that the purpose of the justice system is to convince criminals to go straight and teach them how to do so. Conservatives support some combination of the first three purposes and dismiss rehabilitation as pointless. Liberals tend to focus on rehabilitation and dismiss punishment for its own sake as illegitimate. In regard to the death penalty, conservatives are often accused of being contradictory or hypocritical, especially in light of their support for the sanctity of life. The difference lies in what is earned and unearned, what is deserved or unjust. Conservatism does not support blindly the existence of *all* life, but instead upholds a regard for *innocent* life. Someone's actions can forfeit the tolerance of a decent society, which has the right to protect its innocent members from the internal threats of criminals as well as from the external threats of enemies. These attitudes toward law enforcement are deeply connected to the conservative view of human nature and social fragility. If we do not accept those two premises, the conservative view of law enforcement is at best unnecessary, and at worst counterproductive or oppressive.

But conservatives don't have just positive feelings toward law enforcement. They also fear rogue police and the intrusion of the state into private affairs, which explains why we hear both anti-police as well as anti-criminal sentiments from conservatives at different times. This is not a contradiction, but a question of balance. Specifically, are you more likely to be hurt by uncontrolled criminals or by rogue police? For most citizens at most times the answer is the first, so the current balance is in favor of more law enforcement rather than less. If that balance shifted, it would be different. Or in a specific place or circumstance it may be different, which explains why conservatives are not driven by a set policy, but by the perceived needs of a decent society. It may be important to note that the perception of criminals rather than cops being more dangerous tends to be shared by people who look middle class and unthreatening; it is not necessarily the perception of people who are poor or different in appearance.

Another example of golden mean thinking is in regard to *state power*. Conservatives are fearful of the government; they also want a powerful state in regard to military, law enforcement, and morality. So which is it, do you fear the state or like the state? The answer is *Yes*. Again it is a question of balance. The fear comes from the power of the state to take away individual dignity. Collective schemes generally degrade liberty for little in return. But a strong government is needed in order to maintain security, support property rights, and sometimes to encourage moral behavior among the young and impressionable. Conservatives are often accused of being contradictory on this account: either you like the state or fear it, but you can't do both. Actually, you can. This is only a contradiction if we accept the argument that state power is the central question: you either favor government or oppose it. Conservatives simply have a different principle of ordered liberty. It is just not as easy to explain in a simple sound bite. Under this principle, sometimes the state should be strong and sometimes it should be weak, depending on the current balance between tyranny and disorder, as well as other factors like whether the specific government action works with or against the basic nature of humans. In a time of chaos we need more government action, but in a time of an overbearing state we need less. "But you don't make sense (according to my principle of state action versus state inaction)," some will say. That's right, but it doesn't make sense to insist that someone be consistent based on *your principle*. They are only hypocritical if they contradict *their own principle*.

It is easy to see why many people think conservatism is simply an opposition to big government, which is not an accurate summary of the ideology. It does not explain the more recent support among some conservatives of a broader government role in morality, or a massive increase in the security state following 9/11, with the growth of the Department of Homeland Security and related intelligence agencies. The answer to this seeming contradiction is the principle that we should be anti-government when government has gone too far, and pro-government where it is too weak to protect us, seeking a golden mean. During the 1970s and 1980s, following the rise of socialist economies in Europe, the long-standing Cold War with Russia, and the broad expansion of the American welfare state and regulatory state, conservative opposition to big government was a central theme.

But that was due to the circumstances of the time. This emphasis weakened and altered focus in the 1990s as many conservatives began to take the opposite view toward moral issues because they perceived that social boundaries had become too weak, leaning us more toward anarchy than statism. The welfare state, government regulation of businesses, and deficit spending became more normal as time went on, lessening opposition from the conservatives who adapted to the new norms. The recent return of the national debt as a major political issue was driven by the large increases in government spending during the last years. The conservative opposition to government is driven more by perceived threat and the rejection of utopian designs than by a flat rejection of the role of the state.

Because balance is the touchstone of conservative thought, this means that reasonable people will disagree on particulars. Balance requires judgment, so even those who want the same result will not share the same view about where we are now. Conservatives who are religious will tend to see the current situation as begging for greater morality, while less religious or irreligious conservatives will tend to perceive a different balance. Conservatism is a more complex ideology than one that only envisions movement in a single direction, such as merely expanding freedom or maximizing material output. It can militate in either direction in order to maintain balance. This approach requires wisdom, balanced judgment, and a recognition of the values that are worth upholding.

Liberty in the conservative worldview is not value-free (the belief that all uses of liberty are equally good). Instead, conservatives envision a value-laden liberty that promotes a decent society. Ordered liberty is valuable because it leads to individual human dignity. The aspect of a dignified life that is currently most vulnerable or in retreat is a matter of disagreement, which means that conservatism requires a wise judgment of current conditions. Even fellow conservatives will not agree on which aspect of society is most vulnerable and how it can be protected, which leads us to the next facet of a conservative worldview: its central question and competing answers.

4

THE CENTRAL QUESTION OF CONSERVATISM

The Glue Problem

To summarize the conservative position so far: humans are problematic; democracy is fragile; utopian fantasies are dangerous distractions; individual liberty is the best state of man; free souls need an environment that nurtures that potential while not allowing it to degrade into a state of license or chaos. This ideal is known as *ordered liberty*, or the proper balance between tyranny and disorder. The conservative vision of what is desired and feared can be summarized in two questions: What do we want? Individual dignity, which requires both liberty and decency. What do we know about humans? They are weak and corrupt, and society is vulnerable. These realizations lead to a serious problem: we want people to be free, and to use that freedom for decent ends that protect the dignity of others, but we know that many of them will use their liberty to prey upon others or degrade society. *How do we hold together a free and fragile society?* This is the *Glue Problem*. What can provide the necessary bond without resorting to illegitimate force, which would destroy the same values we wish to preserve? This is no small question. But we must face it if we wish to protect our society and the individuals within it.

The glue problem arises from a clear-minded assessment of conservative premises and values:

Negative Human Nature + Social Fragility + Ordered Liberty = The Glue Problem

A state of decent freedom is difficult to achieve under these conditions, but it is even more of a problem when we consider the third premise—that utopian solutions are fantasies. There can be no magic answer to the glue problem, only answers that require vigilance and renewed effort by each generation as the forces of decline regroup.

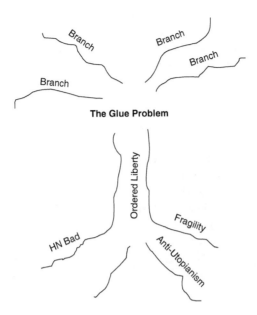

The Glue Problem

Figure 4.1 The Conservative Central Problem

The core of conservatism can be seen as the contradiction between our aspirations to individual liberty and a realistic assessment of the nature of man and society. Question: *When does a state of liberty become a state of license?* Answer: *Quickly and easily.* This can be criticized as a contradictory worldview. Why believe these things that are incompatible? The answer is because they are accurate descriptions. We should try to grasp reality as clearly as possible, regardless of whether what we observe presents a problem. The goal is not to be falsely consistent or foolishly rosy, but to understand things even if they are ugly. It would be easier to see individual liberty and a good society as holding no contradiction, but that would be to deny clear realities of the human condition, and invite decline even faster. In this sense, conservatism is not contradictory; it recognizes that humans are contradictory. We want freedom, but are limited by being corrupt. Conservative thinking merely recognizes this predicament.

The glue problem is the subtext of all conservative thought, even when it is not at the center of the discussion. It explains why conservative politics do not just revolve around the actions of government, but also center on calls for changes in citizen values and a strong role for social institutions outside of government to maintain our collective belief systems. Churches, charities, PTAs, the Boy Scouts, and any number of civic organizations play a crucial role in maintaining civic virtue and social connection. This is especially true in an economy in which upwardly mobile workers and professionals move around the country seeking better opportunities. This improves the financial prospects of individual families, but degrades the attachments to our extended families, our community, and the many organizations and networks that maintained social cohesion in previous generations.

If the glue problem is a non-issue, then questions of morality, patriotism, or other public values are not vital concerns. We can concentrate on literal government policies designed to address specific problems, rather than general goals of stability, decency, or tradition. This will be clearer after seeing the foundations of a liberal worldview, but for now it is sufficient to note that the glue problem is not a worry from the competing ideological perspective. For conservatives, however, the glue problem is the heart of public politics, whether the specific issue at hand is abortion, guns, defense spending, economic redistribution, national healthcare, our response to terrorism, or illegal immigration. In regard to each issue, the conservative response is grounded in the overarching problem of the contradictions between freedom and decency.

As I wrote this in August 2010, I noticed a piece in the *Wall Street Journal* by Peggy Noonan, a well-known conservative who served as a speechwriter for Ronald Reagan. She published an editorial on 6 August entitled "America is at Risk of Boiling Over," which quotes a piece she wrote sixteen years earlier in 1994 on our disunity:

> At home certain trends—crime, cultural tension, some cultural Balkanization—will, we fear, continue; some will worsen. In my darker moments I have a bad hunch. The fraying of the bonds that keep us together, the strangeness and anomie of our popular culture, the increase in walled communities . . . the rising radicalism of the politically correct . . . the increased demand of all levels of government for the money of the people, the spotty success with which we are communicating to the young America's reason for being and founding beliefs, the growth of cities where English is becoming the second language . . . these things may well come together at some point in our lifetimes and produce something painful indeed. I can imagine, for instance, in the year 2020 or so, a movement in some states to break away from the union. Which would bring about, of course, a drama of Lincolnian darkness.

This is a clear representation of the glue problem and the need for national unity.

Conservatives are left with the vital question of how to maintain a free and decent society. *How do we glue together a vulnerable society that values individual liberty?* We need something as a bulwark against decline and disorder, a constant re-stitching of our common threads to stave off the great unravel. But what? The answers to this core question divide conservatism into the ideology's branches.

5

CONSERVATISM
Branches

How do we bind together a free and fragile society so that it does not degrade into indecency, disorder, fading power, and eventual collapse? The prominent answers to this question explain the branches of conservatism. One possible answer is simply hierarchy. We can construct systems of control and authority through strong government powers and rigid social institutions. We counter the threat of disorder by imposing order from above. This may be effective, but it contradicts the conservative desire for the liberty and dignity of the individual. Control by the state destroys freedom, and ceding power to the collective over the individual robs us of dignity. We want individuals to control themselves, not government to do it for them. Most conservatives conclude that the answer of brute power is illegitimate except in dire emergencies. The role of hierarchy in conservative thought is more complex than a wholesale rejection, and we will return to it later, but it is a problematic answer at best. So how do we respond to the glue problem?

The four prominent answers are:

1) patriotism
2) religion
3) property or work ethic, and
4) tradition.

These answers are the heart of National Defense, Social, Economic, and Cultural Conservatism. Each branch provides its own preferred answer, which leads to different central issues and proposed policies. While they often overlap and reinforce each other, each perspective is distinct. Some citizens are attached strongly to one branch of conservatism, while others accept more than one. Some conservatives dispute specific branches as providing false answers, while others embrace all four traditions simultaneously.

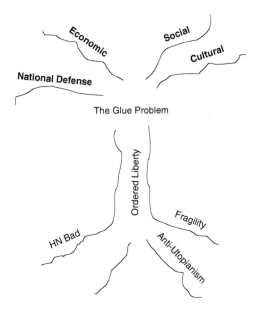

Figure 5.1 Conservative Branches

National Defense Conservatism

If the best answer to the glue problem is *patriotism* as a binding force, this creates National Defense Conservatism. We achieve unity in our defense against external threats. Security is perhaps our most clearly collective goal, in which we all share a common stake. We should therefore embrace the ideal of service to the nation. We should respect our national military institutions and take pride in our young people who choose to serve, whether they are our children, relatives, students, friends, or strangers. We should celebrate the military holidays and rituals. Veterans Day and Memorial Day used to be much more important holidays than they are today. The president still salutes his military guard when boarding Air Force One and on other regular occasions, reflecting his primary constitutional status as the commander in chief. If one reads Article II of the Constitution on the president's powers, it becomes clear that his principal constitutional role is the nation's lead warrior and voice to other nations. George Washington led troops in the field while in office, which would now be unthinkable, but the symbolism remains the same. The West Point motto of Duty, Honor, Country sums up the collective commitments and emotions that maintain a decent society.

Social Conservatism

If the best answer to the glue problem is *religion* as a binding force, this creates Social Conservatism. A common religious heritage in Judeo-Christian traditions, but more importantly a common moral basis, unites us as a society. It provides a foundation for shared goals and perceptions of a decent life. It restrains excessive behavior by providing a sense of personal judgment and public shame. Liberty is much more ordered when it is combined with the recognition of a benevolent but watchful God. Religion is also simply our heritage. The New World was colonized by very religious people and the Protestant tradition has formed much of our collective value system, including a powerful work ethic compared to other nations. The Declaration of Independence is dripping with references to the Divine, including the Founding perception that individual rights to life and liberty were given directly by God; we are free because God imbued us with free will, and are equal because we are all God's children. Our original conception of rights has become more secular over time, and now often relies on the Constitution itself as the sacred source of rights, but we have never fully shifted away from sacredness as the origin, and in an important sense merely made the Constitution sacred.

Dollar bills pass through our hands every day, but most citizens are not familiar with their symbolism. Both sides of the Great Seal of the United States are on the back of every dollar. The front of the seal, on the right, bears the national coat of arms, with its eagle and shield. The Eagle holds an olive branch in one talon and arrows in the other. (This is generally interpreted as an offering of peace, with the assurance that force is ready if peace is rejected.) The back of the Seal is on the left of the dollar. Over the Eye of God at the top of the unfinished pyramid it reads *Annuit coeptis*, Latin for "He watches over us approvingly." The religious symbolism is unmistakable and intentional. President Eisenhower once famously said that "our form of government makes no sense unless it is founded in a deeply felt religious faith, and I don't care what it is." He meant not only that our individual rights derive from Divine sanction, but that a free society requires a moral foundation in order to remain viable. He didn't think it mattered which one because all of our major religious traditions provide this function.

In addition to providing a moral code, our religious traditions are also congregational. We meet in local houses of worship that become social centers as well, fostering cultural and even political unity. Neighborhood black churches are often the center of political as well as social organizing with the African American community. Catholic churches have much more going on than masses, from bingo nights to an expansive school and hospital system. Synagogues come with JCCs and Hillels (community centers and university student groups). The very decentralized constellation of Protestant congregations throughout America are associated with an endless number of study groups, charities, foundations, schools, social movements, and the like. All of this provides a sense of collective fate as well as collective faith. Atheists may have a legitimate belief system, but they don't have bake sales.

In a different sense, the protection that social conservatives seek literally comes from God. Divine Providence watches over us, and without that shield we are vulnerable. This is distinct from the idea that mutual religious traditions and values provide a stable basis for a unified and decent society, but they are entirely compatible.

Economic Conservatism

If the best answer to the glue problem is *property ownership* as a binding force, this creates Economic Conservatism. The binding agents include free markets, a strong work ethic, and competition for excellence, but it is important to understand why property is central. What we own we care about. Home ownership is valued in America far more than in other developed nations. It represents a stake in the community. Citizens who own homes are much more likely to also join neighborhood watches and PTAs, and to care about local politics or the fate of the neighborhood playground. An ownership society promotes stability, the primary conservative goal.

Economic conservatism is also grounded in free markets and open competition. Human excellence is an aspect of individual dignity, and it is revealed only through competition. This is true in academics, sports, and art as well as work. Many people are uncomfortable with competition: it creates winners and losers, resulting in bruised emotions. But an emphasis on competition, rankings, and victory is particularly American and is often noted by visitors and immigrants, many of whom come here for this reason. A recent arrival wrote after he gained citizenship, "My son and I are Americans, we prepare for glory by failing until we don't."[1] Conservatives recognize that the opposite of competition is not cooperation, but hierarchy. If we don't let competitive markets sort it out, it will be done by social caste or corporate monopoly or coercive government. Cooperation rather than

33

competition is the focus of liberal approaches. Markets are undeniably harsh and bruising. But conservatives do not believe that forced cooperation is better, because it will inevitably degrade into coercion and declining performance when individual incentives are removed. We cannot all be winners without winning losing its meaning, because a trophy that everyone gets is no trophy at all. If we attempt to make everyone winners, we all simply lose.

Another aspect of economic conservatism is regard for a strong work ethic. Simply put, work is good. There is an old maxim that idle hands find the Devil's work. In this sense, work ethic is tied to social conservatism, but there is more to it than that. Personal achievement is the core of individual dignity, and we cannot reach a state of self-worth that is not earned. It cannot be given, but only gained.

Aside from valuing competition and achievement, economic conservatives embrace free markets grounded in the anti-utopian premise. Attempts to alter the workings of the market, even when well-intended and seemingly logical, are subject to the law of unintended consequences and the general failings of social engineering. We may want to improve our society, but that is often not what ends up happening.

All of this leads economic conservatives to oppose high taxation in order to fund government spending on entitlement programs such as welfare, long unemployment benefits, national healthcare, and the like. Aside from whether these sorts of government programs are morally justified, another concern is whether they are financially feasible. Citizens in this sub-branch of economic conservatism are often called *fiscal conservatives*, or simply people who focus on the budget. Fiscal conservatives worry more than others that taking out debts in order to fund spending is a degenerate behavior. Economists differ about what the effects of deficit spending and the truly massive federal debt will be in the future, but it can't be good and might be terrible. Currently almost 10 percent of the federal budget goes just to paying the interest on the debt, a figure that is likely to grow dramatically in future years. If the fragility premise holds any currency, it applies not only to foreign enemies and moral decline, but also to unstable spending.

Cultural Conservatism

If the best answer to the glue problem is *tradition* as a binding force, this creates Cultural Conservatism. Some of our most important collective traditions are national ones, our traditions as Americans. A vibrant sense of national identity that trumps other lesser associations is the key to a stable society. Our national motto, also on the Great Seal and the dollar, is

E Pluribus Unum. From Many, One. From many different immigrant nation-alities, religious traditions, and individual concerns, we forge one identity as Americans, which is more important than any other.

This answer to the glue problem has focused many conservatives on illegal immigration as a central concern. The English language itself is a crucial unifying force, not only so we can all communicate, but also because language carries much of our cultural heritage. The large numbers of Mexican immigrants over the past few decades have created Spanish-speaking areas in the border zone of the South and West. Miami has become one of the least English-speaking cities in the United States, culturally more Latin American than American. Over 65 percent of the residents speak Spanish as their primary language, and at least 30 percent cannot conduct a conversation in English. Growing areas of Texas, New Mexico, Arizona, and southern California are heading in the same direction. Unchecked illegal immigration from Mexico creates the specter of a divided nation within a few generations, one part English-speaking and the other Spanish. Much like Canada's division between the British and French provinces, and the recurring political movement to secede by the Québécois, we may become a split nation. If we go in the same direction, we too will become divided, bickering, and consequently weak, like Kanuckistan.

Cultural conservatives are not only concerned about national traditions, but also social ones. Tradition, in and of itself, regardless of the specific content, is good because it unifies us around known customs and regular events. This is why cultural conservatives object to the corporate regularization of "Happy Holidays" rather than "Merry Christmas." Non-Christians can have a merry Christmas as well, and being invited to join the national tradition is not an insult but quite the opposite. Traditional relations among husbands and wives, men and women, parents and children are also a central concern. Hundreds of years of human experience have demonstrated that traditional family structures are a good thing. The collective research from social science makes clear that being raised in a single-parent household is a strong predictor of every known social pathology, including crime, drug addiction, early pregnancies, interrupted education, and life-long poverty.

This does not mean we should discriminate against anyone who does not come from a traditional family background, but it means that we should not encourage or normalize alternative arrangements. Traditional gender roles should be respected and promoted for those women who choose to emphasize family, and for those men who choose to embrace their responsibilities as protectors. One of the little-noted aspects of female equality has been the abandonment by men of their traditional roles to protect or even respect women; if they are equal now, many young males think, then I have no responsibility toward them at all.

Gay marriage is perhaps the most vocalized current issue of tradition versus alternatives. Again it is not a matter of discrimination against individuals, but an appreciation of marriage as a specific thing that is not open to renegotiation. If one does not wish to join the institution as it is, this does not mean it should be altered to accommodate other desires. The conservative desire to respect gender roles and nuclear families is not merely because they are a unifying force in society, but also because they reflect valued traits that we admire: femininity and masculinity are, in a word, good, reflecting beauty and caring, or strength and courage. Gender neutrality is something else, and we need not admire it.

We sometimes hear the terms social and cultural conservatism interchanged, or the term cultural conservative used for social conservatives. The ideology is often described as having only three branches (national defense, economic, and social). But it is important to distinguish between cultural and social conservatives. The two branches are somewhat similar and individual citizens are often both, but they have different core concerns. Even when the two perspectives agree on a given issue, it is for different reasons, one grounded in religion and the other in tradition. On gay marriage, both agree that the recent movement has been in the wrong direction, but one for religious reasons of sin and the other because it upsets tradition and older virtues. Cultural conservatives are not as concerned about abortion, while social conservatives are not as concerned about illegal immigration. This is especially true because Mexican immigrants tend to be more religious than native-born citizens, giving social and cultural conservatives different perspectives.

The conservative branch that is more prominent at a given time often reflects the current circumstances or ongoing public discussions. It depends on what is perceived to be out of balance. With the rise of the welfare state and the regulatory state following World War II, along with the rise of the communist movement and the Soviet challenge, economic and national defense conservatism were dominant. The success of the women's movement, the sexual revolution, and now the gay rights movement has altered the balance toward social conservatism. The rise of illegal immigration and multiculturalism in recent years has bolstered cultural conservatism.

Table 5.1 illustrates the four conservative branches and their competing ideals. Each can be summarized in a clear slogan. To national defense conservatives, "It's A Dangerous World," which is really all one needs to know.

Table 5.1 Conservative Branches

Branch	Summary	Central Value	Central Issues
National Defense	It's a Dangerous World	militarism v. pacifism	war, military budget, response to terrorism
Social	God is Great	religiosity v. secularism	abortion, gay marriage
Economic	You Keep What You Earn	individualism v. communitarianism	taxation, welfare state, national health care
Cultural	Tradition is Good	tradition v. openness, nationalism v. internationalism	illegal immigration

For social conservatives, "God is Great," while for economic conservatives, "You Keep What You Earn." Cultural conservatives know that "Tradition is Good," which again covers a large waterfront. The branches focus on different values and issues. Even when they agree with the policy positions of other branches, their own concerns are primary. For national defense conservatives it is support for necessary military actions and strong responses to terrorism; for social conservatives it is abortion and gay marriage that are most worrisome; to economic conservatives it is overburdening taxation and spending on the welfare state and national health care; while for cultural conservatives it is illegal immigration. If each group had to choose only one thing on which they could have their way, those would be the choices.

A few final notes center on how the branches of conservatism relate to each other. The different conservative perspectives are most often mutually reinforcing. Regardless of differences in focus, it is natural for conservative citizens to resonate with more than one branch of the ideology. Strong and clear connections exist between any one branch of conservatism and the rest. In a sense, the primary form of the ideology that leads to each of the other branches may be national defense conservatism. If we value a strong defense grounded in national unity, then economic conservatism provides more of the financial and material output necessary for our defense, social conservatism encourages a unified society that can stand up for itself, and cultural conservatism supports national identification and traditions of respect for service. Aside from national defense concerns leading to additional conservative perspectives, there are strong links among the other branches as well. Social and cultural conservatism are focused on several of the same issues. Social and economic conservatism are tied together through the Protestant backing of the work ethic. Evangelical thought in particular reinforces the idea of wealth accumulation and the value of being productive (sometimes known as the wealth gospel). Social conservatism is tied to military service because both emphasize sacrifice for the group rather than personal interests. Cultural conservatism increases support for the military through its regard for national identification. But the most important way in which the different branches are linked is that citizens who are looking for social unity can find it in several dimensions that are mutually reinforcing.

This is not to say that there are no arguments within the clan. Conflict emerges when it comes to leadership within the Republican Party, especially over presidential nominations. John McCain is a perfect example of a conservative who adheres to some branches but not others. He is only a national defense and economic conservative in earnest. His views are suspect to social conservatives, and not trusted by cultural conservatives. He made peace with the religious in order to gain the nomination in 2008, but they knew that he was not truly one of them. An important observation is that George W. Bush represented all four branches of conservatism. One of the reasons he gained immediate and decisive support over McCain for the 2000 nomination was that he appealed to all of the branches and alienated none. Sarah Palin is also all four.

One of the common disagreements within the ideology is between national defense conservatives and others. As noted above, being a warhawk might lead to supporting the other views, but the reverse is not the case. Warfighting is expensive, which brings those who are more worried about the national debt into conflict with those who are pro-war. There is also a streak of isolationism among some conservatives, which brings them into conflict with contemporary pro-war conservatives. (This will be discussed more fully in Chapter 14.) An important disagreement can arise between the purely economic conservatives and the rest. Businessmen who are more socially liberal, and sometimes more pacifistic (war is generally bad for business, unless you are in the right kind of business), tend to dispute national defense and social conservatives. Economic conservatism is also more individualistic, while the other two perspectives require more of a sense of sacrifice for the group.

Another noteworthy source of division among conservatives is the role of privilege or hierarchy. Privilege may be a form of tyranny, but is also the result of individual liberty. The question is where the proper balance lies. A part of the problem is that wealthy people have every incentive to maintain their wealth and privilege across generations. This impulse is merely hierarchy, not a conservative concern for ordered liberty or social stability. But the wealthy will line up with conservatives simply out of self-interest rather than principle. In this sense it is important to distinguish between principled conservatism and the self-interest of wealth. This explains why many liberals who have family money oppose inheritance taxes while taking liberal positions on other political questions, in violation of their principles but in favor of their pockets. This is not them being conservative, but merely following their self-interest.

There is a sense, however, in which conservatism and hierarchy are connected in principle. Hierarchy is an old answer to the glue problem, much older than free market capitalism and broad-based ownership of property, much older than liberal democracy itself. Enough hierarchy is a golden mean answer if the hierarchy creates stability without costing too much in dominance. Where we think that balance lies is influenced by our answer to the question: "Are wealthy people virtuous?" This may seem an odd question, but if the privileged use their power for good ends, it may not be a bad thing to allow them greater influence. The older argument in favor of aristocracy was that nobles were chosen by God for their position, and who are we to interfere? More to the point, they had a sense of *noblesse oblige*, or the responsibility to serve society in return for their position. The modern argument is that the wealthy are a natural aristocracy: they are better educated, more cultured, and born to a sense of responsibility. Other contemporary observers note that the sense of moral obligation of wealth is no longer prevalent among the children of upper-class families, and the elite prep schools are filled with drug use and hedonism rather than a sense of duty. When we ask where you find the best people in American society, some believe that the answer is still in exclusive gated communities. Others believe it is among the patriots in military service, especially those from the service academies like West Point and Annapolis, which are some of the hardest universities in America to enter and pass, in intellectual, physical, and moral terms. Others believe that individuals of great intelligence, strength, morality, and drive are randomly distributed throughout society, though often without the resources necessary to achieve as much success and add as much to society as those from wealthier backgrounds. Others believe the question itself is irrelevant or oddly elitist. That final group are rarely conservatives, who tend to see the question as important in choosing our leaders, but often disagree on the answer.

Different views toward hierarchy and privilege remain a source of disagreement among conservatives. Some accept a broader role for wealthy and powerful individuals and families as natural leaders. Others see this as a form of corruption and embrace a more populist form of conservatism that trusts the instincts of middle-brow citizens over the privileged authority of the wealthy. An important question is the role of inheritance. A system that emphasizes free markets and property means that individuals born into wealthy families will have a substantial leg up on others in the competition, because of advantages in education, financing to start business enterprises, and contacts among influential people. This is where conservatism can become hierarchy, or unearned privilege. One way of framing the question is whether a family handout is as corrupting as a government handout. If the answer is yes, then we emphasize real personal accomplishments; it is individual work and achievement that is ennobling, not gifts that come from random accidents of birth. This leads some conservatives to side with liberals in favoring inheritance taxes, which remove some of the unearned privileges of birth. But many conservatives consider this form of taxation to be as bad as others, or even more so as an attempt at social engineering that takes away one's right to provide for your own children. This led to the common name of a "death tax," focusing on the parents, rather than inheritance taxes being known as a "rich kid tax," focusing on the children, or a "Paris Hilton tax," focusing on the undeserving.

Like the answer to the glue problem, the problem of inheritance divides conservatives. One way of understanding the divide has to do with different cultural definitions of the individual. We speak of individual rights and personal accomplishments, but the original conception of a free man included his wife and children as an extension of himself. As we moved away from male-dominated households and more strict family structures, we embraced a more truly individual conception of the person. But we have never fully divorced family connections from our thinking. Conservatives who see inheritance as natural still see a person as enmeshed in their family origin, something that simply cannot and should not be altered. Conservatives who see inheritance as disrupting the system of free market competition for status and wealth tend to think of individuals as free-standing persons, and birth as an unearned accident that randomly advantages some and disadvantages others with no regard for virtue. If being pro-market means keeping everything *your family* earns, then inheritance taxes are bad; if being pro-market means keeping everything *you* earn, then inheritance taxes are good.

While conflicts among conservatives occur, they have far more common ground than opposing ideals. The great majority of the time there is little that keeps conservatives from supporting each other's policies, and nothing that stops them from banding together against ideological opponents. One answer may be sufficient, but many conservatives embrace two, three, or all four answers to the glue problem.

Part II

LIBERALISM

6

LIBERALISM

Premise Foundations

Liberalism begins with distinct ways of understanding humans and society. Individually we are meant for growth and collectively we are capable of improvement. Perhaps *capable* is the wrong word; it may not be too strong to say *destined*, if we have enough trust in each other and will to stay the course until a better world arrives. Change is inevitable. The only question is whether we will embrace and shape those changes in order to create a better society.

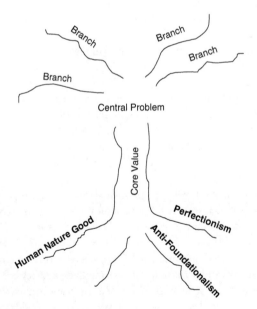

Figure 6.1 Liberal Premises

Perfectionism

Perhaps the most influential liberal premise about humans and society is that both can be perfected. We can build, inspire, and become something better than what we currently are. Is our society limited to what we know and have seen? The answer is a resounding *No*. More importantly, are we limited to what *we* are and have been? Humans can change, as well as society changing. Perfectionism applies not only to governments, organizations, or social norms, but also to people. Over the last centuries we have become better educated, more tolerant, more in touch with our capacities for creativity, and we will continue to improve, as long as our will is not sapped or our energies diverted.

This sentiment toward change and perfection is clear in the language of the most noteworthy liberal political programs of our history: FDR's New Deal and LBJ's Great Society. Each phrase evokes a vision of a better world: a New one, a Great one. Bobby Kennedy expressed the same belief with one of his signature phrases, which also ended the eulogy given by his brother Ted Kennedy after Bobby's assassination in 1968: "As he said many times, in many parts of this nation. . . . Some men see things as they are and say, Why? I dream things that never were and say, Why not?"

Barack Obama's 2008 campaign slogan "Yes We Can" is grounded in the same concept. When President Obama appeared on *The Daily Show* right before the 2010 midterm elections, becoming the first sitting president to do so, the first question Jon Stewart put to him was, "So here you are, you're two years in to your administration, and the question that arises in my mind: are we the people we were waiting for?" The audience as well as the president chuckled politely, because Stewart was making fun of the exaggerated expectations of the first years of the Obama presidency, which contributed to the liberal disillusionment and lack of enthusiasm prior to the tremendous midterm losses to the Republicans, but he was also invoking the basic premise of liberalism: not are *you* as president what we were waiting for, but have *we* become what we should be.

The underlying question of this premise is about our perception of human effort and action. Is it worthwhile or pointless? Are we active creatures who can shape our world, or are we powerless in the face of forces beyond our control? Do we believe that our public works are good? Mistakes happen (and can be corrected), but human effort leads to improvements, like more schools, hospitals, and parks that improve our lives, and better social institutions that protect our weaker members. Human plans beat natural forces or random events. Our ideas, dreams, and works lead to good things.

Perhaps a better way to phrase this is not whether our efforts are fruitful or pointless, but whether the world can be different. The belief that we can change things requires at a deeper level the belief that the world can change. The opposite perception is that the world is static in important ways: Even if it does change or evolve, this is not done by our design. In this opposing view, prevailing conditions or social institutions that exist naturally are better than things we create. Both humans and society are what they are, and resist our attempts to mold them. But human societies clearly *do* change. And we have been responsible for many of the positive changes. These include the creation of public school systems that allow all of our young people to attend rather than only a few; a system of higher education that is the envy of the world, supported heavily by public funding for research and government loans for middle-class and poor students; a society far more open to the achievement of women and minorities; much more widely available health care; a safety net for the truly poor; financial markets with less volatility and lower likelihood of crashing than they had fifty or a hundred years ago, and one could go on.

All of these things were the result of planning rather than market forces. We can choose to trust that markets will generate unguided but nonetheless positive outcomes, what Adam Smith called the Invisible Hand. But the Invisible Hand of the market often gives us the finger. Things in our society will be organized by someone, but maybe not for the greater good. We can organize things ourselves, or allow the negative motives of greed, exploitation, and dominance to do the organizing for us.

Perhaps another way to understand this premise goes beyond the efficacy of our actions or the malleability of society, and is instead a statement of hope. This can be thought of as an acceptance of risk for a future payoff, or a dismissal of pessimism about human potential. At the 1936 Democratic convention, when FDR was running for his second term as president, he said,

> Divine justice weights the sins of the cold blooded and the sins of the warm hearted on different scales. Better the occasional fault of a government in the spirit of charity than the consistent omission of a government in the ice of its own indifference.

The goal of Roosevelt's New Deal was to create a safety net for those who were unable to prosper in a market economy, and the goal of Lyndon Johnson's Great Society was to no longer have a permanent under-class by breaking the cycle of poverty for a generation. The more lofty the goal, the less successful each attempt was, but they succeeded in boldly experimenting. We don't have to know something is going to work to know it is something worth working for. Any failures are noble ones, while any achievements are a legacy for a better future. Is it more arrogant to think you can change the world, or more cowardly to think you shouldn't try?

Human Nature

Perfectionism relies on the ability of government to aggregate the goodwill of individuals. This rests on the belief that the will of most citizens is in fact good. A positive view of human nature is a bedrock of the liberal worldview. Disputing the conservative view that humans are innately aggressive, the liberal premise is that this behavior is not natural or innate but the result of circumstance, usually deprivation or oppression. The common, and natural, state of man is peaceful, cooperative, and willing to see a common interest.

Perhaps rather than seeing human nature as inherently cooperative rather than combative, the more modern take is that human nature does not really exist. The concept is a remnant of older thinking that insists on categorizing people as X or Y in an immutable sense. Humans may simply be more malleable than predestined. We are the products of our environment, and could easily go either way. Even thinking in terms of human nature is something of a mistake. This means that you are not a good person because you were simply born that way. And maybe other people we perceive as bad were not born *that* way, but were shaped by negative influences that we didn't have to face. Maybe they weren't born bad, but made that way.

If human nature is more changeable than static, social institutions become all the more important, especially for children. If character is constructed, it can be reconstructed. Earlier we mentioned the disagreement in Western philosophy between Hobbes and Rousseau over the basic nature of man. Rousseau is the great champion of goodness being innate and corruption being caused by society. It is not a coincidence that he considered his most important book to be *Emile, or On Education*, a fictional account of the influences on a child's development. The first sentence is "Everything is good as it leaves the hands of the Author of things; everything degenerates in the hands of man." The second point is perhaps more important than the first, as so much of the negative in the world is socially constructed. This is in direct contrast to the perception that natural or unguided outcomes are superior. What is superior about the poverty, violence, crime, pressure to conform, instability of the economy, and ruthless anxiety that plagues human society? Are we destined to live in Hobbes' state of nature, in which human life remains nasty and brutish, or can we change our society to accord with our potential?

We should ask ourselves: Are things better now, or fifty years ago? Will things likely be better fifty years in the future, or will they likely be worse? Few rational people would choose the more constricted, less educated, poorer, and shorter lives that Americans lived fifty years ago. And we should have a similar faith that people and things will continue to get better in the future if we do not abandon the same collective efforts that brought us out of the past. Perhaps the clearest way of phrasing the distinctions between conservative and liberal premises is whether they lead us to emphasize *protecting versus perfecting* society. Is our primary goal insulating us from decline or preparing us for improvement? This is the heart of the disagreement.

Anti-Foundationalism

The third liberal premise is quite different from the other two. While the premises we have mentioned up to this point are clear claims to knowledge, this one is the reverse—a denial of what we can know. Anti-foundationalism is the *rejection of foundations of knowledge or absolute truths*. It is the argument that we can't know that one truth or value is the appropriate starting point. This is sometimes confused with relativism, or the view that all values are equally good, but liberals are not really relativists. They don't start from the position that we can't know that one value is better than another, because they do have certain core values. Instead, liberals believe that we can't know which truth to start from. Therefore we have to grant each perspective its own share of respect. The value this leads to is tolerance, or the acceptance of multiple views in a non-judgmental atmosphere. It also supports equality as a core value, because we cannot know for sure which view is best, so we must promote equality among people, creeds, and cultures. This is not relativism per se, because it does lead to strong value commitments (to tolerance and equality). It simply does not start from an unquestionable value position, but instead arrives there from a different direction.

Anti-foundationalism has strong roots in contemporary academics, a facet of the interwoven nature of liberalism and academia.[1] The premise is also connected to another powerful movement of the contemporary academy known as *post-modernism*, which rejects traditional methods of knowing. Post-modernism is grounded in the view that human observation is faulty and biased, and therefore cannot be trusted. How one person observes and interprets a given event may be entirely different from how another person sees it. As Anaïs Nin famously said, "We don't see things as *they* are;

we see things as *we* are." Who are we to judge who is correct? Traditional methods that rely on trusting the observations of trained authorities just engrain certain biases. Therefore, knowledge is what post-modernists call *perspectival*, which means that we each have our own perspective from which we understand things; all are equally, or at least somewhat, valid. One does not need to take anti-foundationalism or post-modernism to extremes to see that they have a point about the uncertainty of knowledge and absolute values, as well as the questionable decency of forcing received wisdom on everyone else.

These perspectives lead to a general distrust of Western roots and a recognition of the dark side of our heritage. This includes a history of slavery, religious warfare, exclusion of others from power and status, the exploitation of nature, and imperialism (both literal imperialism in the historical capture of colonies and cultural imperialism in the continued dominance over other groups). It is questionable to be proud of such traditions. It is also not easy to assume that American ways or values are better than others. This makes liberals uncomfortable with gut-level patriotism, which seems tinged with dominance, intolerance, and arrogance.

When we think about how the premise of anti-foundationalism fits with the previous two, it may not be immediately clear. The premises of perfectionism and a positive view of human nature are mutually reinforcing. Humans are destined for improvement in part because they are good to begin with, and those improved social circumstances will make us better because we are innately malleable. Humans improve society, and society can improve humans. The wildcard seems to be anti-foundationalism. In a sense it even seems contradictory: If we do not have an absolute value or a starting point from which to know what is better or worse, how can we say what form of society will be better, or what is really an improvement? If we can't say with certainty what is good, how can we know when a malleable human nature leads to positive outcomes? But this is a superficial criticism, which does not follow the meaning and ramifications of anti-foundationalism to where it really leads. The premise sets up a specific way of understanding what we can and cannot know. And therefore what we can and cannot judge. The academic word for this is *epistemology*, which means the foundations of knowledge. The point is that liberals and conservatives understand knowledge very differently, grounded in their specific premises. This allows anti-foundationalism to play an important role that reinforces the other two liberal premises.

Liberals and conservatives reach different conclusions about what can be known and what cannot. For liberals, what *can* be know is how to improve society.

This is the direct result of perfectionism and a positive or malleable view of human nature. This kind of knowledge is within the range of human intellect and perhaps more importantly, human experience, as we attempt to alter our world. In conservative epistemology, the consequences of government action or interference with the natural order are exactly what we *cannot* know. This conclusion is the direct result of anti-utopianism, a negative view of human nature, and social fragility. We can meddle with things, but this will have unpredictable results as the system adjusts to go back to its natural order, and the inflexible nature of man reasserts itself (the law of unintended consequences). The results are unknowable, but likely negative.

For conservatives, the clearest thing that *can* be known is right versus wrong, or good versus bad. We have clear standards and authoritative traditions to guide us on these questions. In this sense, *conservatives are ruthless categorizers, while liberals resist the process of pigeon-holing people.* Liberal question: "Who is to say what is right or wrong?" Conservative answer: "*We* are." "But why do you think you can make those judgments, to say what is better or worse, who is deserving and who is not?" Conservatives offer two distinct answers to that question. One is elitist: we are educated people, who have thought about these vital questions. The second is populist: we are moral people, who have a clear sense of these vital questions. While there are tensions between the more elitist and populist justifications, both approaches accept that judgments can and must be made in a decent society.

	Can Know	Can't Know
Conservative	good v. bad right v. wrong	consequences of government action
Liberal	how to improve society	absolute values

Figure 6.2 Conservative and Liberal Knowledge

For liberals, this is exactly the sort of knowledge that we *cannot* have. We cannot know which values are absolute or which traditions are the true bedrock. We only have competing perspectives and valid beliefs, which must all be respected. Anti-foundationalism means that a decent society must *not* emphasize judgment, but instead uphold tolerance. If we cannot *know*, we must be *tolerant*. We must recognize the equality of competing values, perspectives, and cultures. The conclusion derived from anti-foundationalism is not uncertain relativism, but certainty that we must be tolerant and must promote equality. It provides a view of what a better society is like, which dovetails with perfectionism and a positive view of human nature. A more perfect society embodies tolerance and equality, in public attitudes as well as in public policies. Our goal should be a better society, comprised of good people, who do not rush to judge. Together these premises lead directly to the core value of liberalism, what can be summarized as *social justice*.

7

THE CORE VALUE
OF LIBERALISM

Social Justice

The liberal premises create an optimistic worldview grounded in the prospect of a better future. Humans are good when given a chance, and society is improvable in ways that will offer that opportunity. But the flip side of being optimistic about the future is being critical of the present. The idea that humans are born innocent and corrupted by society suggests that our society is corrupt in important ways. The liberal premises highlight the

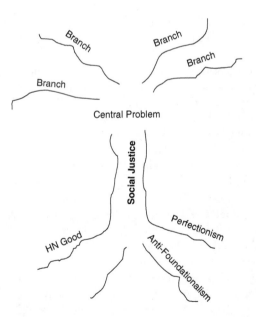

Figure 7.1 Liberal Core Value

failings of contemporary society and a vision of a more just order. This means breaking forms of oppression, resulting in social justice.

The concept of oppression has many facets and origins, but can be traced to a famous observation that "man is born free, but everywhere he is in chains" (the opening lines of Rousseau's *Social Contract*). This thought evolved over the past two hundred years into a strong commitment to alleviating the impersonal forces that limit personal advancement. These forces include discrimination of various kinds (based on race, gender, ethnicity, religion, sexuality, or other differences), poverty, imperialism, class systems, or any other institution or belief system that denies individuals their free and equal place in society, or convinces them to acquiesce in its denial. Social justice is the alleviation of oppression. It is the creation of an individually free and socially equal society.

The core value of social justice is intimately connected to the three liberal premises. People are good or have the potential for goodness (positive human nature), while the social forces that hold them down can be changed because humans and society are improvable rather than static (perfectionism). We don't know exactly what are the best beliefs that they ought to hold (anti-foundationalism), so we must elevate society by not only increasing human potential but also establishing tolerance for human difference. Therefore we must actively shape a more free and equal society—free from oppression and intolerance, and equal in political influence and economic prospects.

This creates a vision of a good society remarkably different from the conservative goal of a more stable and decent social order. The good society is a more just one. It recognizes the human potential to grow rather than the human urge to hunker down with what we already have. It is important to realize that only in a conservative worldview is a just and equal society any contradiction to a stable and decent one. Only a state of significant social fragility would create this tension. In an important sense, justice *creates* stability, and equality is a form of decency. Without the fragility assumption, the concept of ordered liberty is an odd formulation, not really understandable within the liberal framework. To liberals, freedom is value-free, meaning that it can be used for whatever the individual desires as long as it does not hurt others directly. This conception of freedom is very different from the conservative way of understanding liberty, in which freedom is value-laden as opposed to value-free. In the conservative view, rights are tied to responsibilities, so liberty is connected intimately to values, or a best set of choices. In the liberal conception of liberty, we can't tell anyone else what to think or be—how they should limit their liberty in order to be a good citizen—because this is not only a contradiction, but a form of oppression. The only way to avoid the logical trap of being oppressive in order to advance liberty is to insist on a system of full freedoms, backed by an equal regard for different legitimate outcomes. This is one of several ways that liberals and conservatives misunderstand each other because their competing premises do not allow the opposing worldview to make sense. Without the fragility premise, the conservative insistence that a stable society is more important than an increasingly just one sounds nonsensical. To conservatives, the idea that social experiments do not have meaningful costs and risks is equally nonsensical. The conservative view that ordered liberty rather than pure liberty is the best goal sounds to liberals like a flat contradiction, even an intentional one. Without an appreciation for the conservative premises, especially fragility, it is easy to conclude that conservatives are simply masking their true intent to oppress. From the perspective of the liberal premises, this is not only unnecessary but violates the core value of social justice.

With this in mind we can begin to see why the conservative worldview is more offensive to liberals than the liberal worldview offends conservatives. From the perspective of social justice, ordered liberty sounds like oppression, a direct violation of the core value. It is an unnecessary violation, and therefore most likely driven simply by self-interest and a will to dominate. From the perspective of ordered liberty, social justice sounds like a high-minded but foolish ideal. It is likely the product of not understanding the harsher realities and limits of the world, and therefore the real costs and trade-offs. It is wrong-headed, but not the willful misdeed of bad people. It is more error than evil. But the liberal worldview leads to seeing conservatives as perhaps the opposite. To liberals, conservatives are bad people. It is their greed and close-mindedness that is to blame. To conservatives, on the other hand, liberals are simply dumb, but it is their high-minded un-realism that makes them that way. The assessment of the opposing camps is far from symmetrical. We will return to this point later, but the distinction in how each core value influences perceptions of the other ideology is one of the central reasons that conservatives and liberals misunderstand each other.

The core value of social justice leads liberals to focus on three things: *equality*, *group (as well as individual) orientation*, and *responsive government*. But perhaps the central emphasis is on equality. While ordered liberty as a core value leads to the goal of individual dignity, social justice as a core value leads to the goal of equality. In the broadest sense this means the equal worth of individuals. It also means equal political power, which enables the weaker members of society to resist oppression by more powerful citizens across a range of issues. It means equal access to the routes toward achievement and advancement, especially education and jobs. It means equal economic standing, or at least a minimum floor of economic support for all members of society. It also means equal respect, not merely for individuals, but for groups, cultures, and creeds. This is one reason liberalism focuses on group as well as individual conceptions of identity. I am equally respected, my group is equally respected, and my beliefs are equally respected.

It is important to note how much this contrasts with the conservative worldview, which is grounded in the assumption that all beliefs cannot possibly be equal because they uphold different values and result in different outcomes that are very much not equally good. Different views may have an equal right to exist, but to pretend they are equally worthy of public respect is wrong. It is very important to see this distinction, because it explains why so much of contemporary politics is symbolic. Many of our public debates are not about specific policies or government actions, but instead about public respect. For example, in many ways the gay marriage debate is not about equal access to economic advantages or visiting rights in hospitals, which have been achieved by existing laws or could be achieved by civil unions. Instead it is about equal respect as much as equal rights, about whether gay marriages—and hence homosexual relationships—are considered normal and equal in our everyday language.

While a core value of liberty leads toward a focus on the individual, an emphasis on equality creates a *group orientation*. To be clear, liberals are also concerned about individual rights, but have a stronger focus on group identities than is natural for conservatives. Equality is by nature a comparison to the social norm. It only has meaning when we compare an individual to the group, or one group to another. Social justice is primarily focused on historically oppressed groups, including African Americans, women, immigrants (in contemporary America often Hispanics), homosexuals, the poor, or the handicapped. This encourages citizens to identify with their specific social group, especially in terms of race, gender, ethnicity, etc. The economic or social status of the *group* is an important focus, while conservatives concentrate more on individual outcomes. The liberal worldview is less comfortable with competition, markets, or the idea of winners and losers in society. The goal of forging community trumps the concept of individual competition.

Equality is something the group offers rather than something you take. This requires an emphasis on collective action. This can only be achieved if we have *responsive government*. Only then can we harness the power of the state for positive ends. Government is nothing more than the aggregate

SOCIAL JUSTICE

goodwill of citizens. It is our best means of achieving greater equality and tolerance, especially when powerful interests attempt to block change. At a deeper level, the role of government is not just a matter of effectiveness, but of shared responsibility. We are collectively as well as individually responsible for the welfare of citizens. Because human nature is malleable, positive outcomes for individual citizens are dependent on positive circumstances within society. Each person must have a minimum level of affluence and stability, freedom from want and worry. Otherwise we will not have productive and peaceful citizens, and much of the discord will be due to our misguided policies.

We must recognize our shared responsibility for individual outcomes. We are neither solely in charge of our success nor solely to blame for our failings. From the beginning of our lives, our social circumstances shape our beliefs, ambitions, talents, and opportunities. Our own work got us to where we are, but it was not *only* our own work. And their own failings may have brought some of us down, but maybe not merely their own choices. One of the most divisive questions underlying American politics is "Whose fault is it?" From the perspective of rugged individualism, we may each face problems and it might be difficult, but nonetheless the responsibility lies with each of us alone to succeed or fail. This is easy to say when we are not facing large problems. It is usually said by people who grew up very middle class or above, with supportive families and good schools. Under these conditions it is easy to remember our own hard work and easy to forget the family support, financial backing, time to study, good teachers, and clear examples that helped us along the way. Perhaps we should have a shared sense of responsibility for social ills and personal failings. What is the root of crime? Is it merely evil intent and personal weakness? Or is it, perhaps, poverty, homelessness, and the negative examples and psychological damages of growing up in a poor environment, combined with the lack of positive examples that pave the way to optimism and success? The same question applies to why people fall into drug addiction, or why we have such divisions in wealth and status between whites and blacks. How much of the history, of individuals and groups, do we take into account, or how much do we insist that an individual's fate is their own doing? In a competitive world, one can screw up, but one can also get screwed, which introduces a large element of luck and chance that we can try to reduce.

One way of assessing opportunity in America is whether individuals have multiple chances or a single chance. Poor people do have a chance in America, but usually only one. Middle-class and wealthy people have multiple chances. Fail out of school? No problem, just go to another one. Get

55

pregnant young? No problem, we will provide resources or raise the child while you stay in school. Get caught using drugs or driving drunk? No problem, we'll get a lawyer, pay the fine, and move on. Need rehab for that addiction? That will be taken care of too. Therapy for a psychological difficulty? The problems go on, but the answer is the same. That answer is absent for people who start below the middle-class line, and any number who have a great deal of native ability simply don't make it beyond a personal failing, random accident, medical problem, or family emergency that derails them. Can you make it in America if you start poor but are intelligent, hard-working, and virtuous? Definitely yes. But you better be all of those things. Any failing can bring things to a halt. But if you have family backing, several faults will not stop you.

Some of the best American policies of the twentieth century were liberal attempts to expand the second chances available to all Americans. These include the G.I. Bill and college loan programs, which radically changed higher education after World War II from the province of the wealthy to a broad avenue of advancement across America, opening the professions to lower middle-class people. The Civil Rights Act of 1964 and the decisions of the Supreme Court in that era opened education and opportunity to minorities, radically expanding the second chances of non-whites. Medicare and Medicaid provided healthcare for elderly and impoverished Americans and most importantly for poor children. The recent changes in health care under the Obama administration will further expand the availability of basic health to all Americans rather than only those with insurance coverage through their employers. These are movements toward social justice, lowering the barriers to individual and group equality, but we are a long way from the goal.

8

THE CENTRAL QUESTION OF LIBERALISM
The Oppression Problem

To summarize the liberal position so far: Human nature is more malleable than static, which means that we are imbued with great potential for good. Both society and individuals are destined for improvement. We cannot be sure which values are absolutes, so we must encourage tolerance and equality among beliefs and traditions. This provides us with a vision of a better society: a more free and equal world. Inequality and intolerance infect many aspects of our culture, but they can be eliminated through wise policies that harness the collective goodwill of citizens. This eradication of oppression is known as Social Justice, or the steady destruction of the impersonal forces that limit personal advancement. In this way we can perfect our society through our collective efforts.

We often hear the term "Progressive" applied to contemporary liberals. This became much more common after "Liberal" became a term of attack by Republicans in the presidential elections of the late 1980s and 1990s, as well as in the recent campaigns against George W. Bush's opponents Al Gore and John Kerry. In some ways it is a description used to avoid the more obvious term. But it is not merely a euphemism, as it emphasizes the aspect of liberalism grounded in the pursuit of social progress. The question of course is what is meant by progress? For conservatives, progress does not mean anything new or different, but instead can only be a return to earlier values and the principles of the Founding. For liberals, progress is defined by something new, the alleviation of oppression.

This takes us to the central question of liberalism. Just as the glue problem is the limiting factor of conservatism, or the point at which the ideology runs into an internal contradiction that can only be solved by competing possible answers, the central question of liberalism is the *Oppression Problem*. The heart of the matter and source of disagreement is *Who is oppressed?* Who

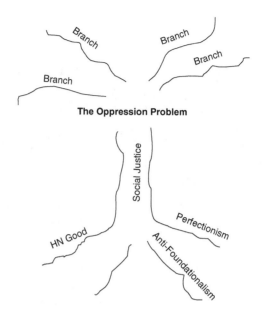

Figure 8.1 The Liberal Central Problem

is oppressed more? Who is oppressed the most? This is the limiting factor that begins to divide liberal intentions, resources, and supporters.

The natural problem of progressivism is where to progress first. Where do we focus resources? Which social ills take priority? Priorities are unavoidable because of limited budgets as well as limited space on the public agenda. Democratic politics is inherently constrained by the attention of the public and the media. There is only so much space on CNN and in our political discussion. One can try to deny there are limits to the good we can do, that we can give all of our social ills equal weight and address all of them simultaneously. But this idea disappears as soon as we confront the political realities of budgets, attention, support, and time. Choices must be made and people will not agree on those choices.

One might think the central question of liberalism would be how to rectify oppression. Interestingly, it is not. The policy answers are clear and noncontroversial among liberals, so the suggested solutions are not divisive. The answer to poverty? Shift income from high and middle to low (the welfare state). Discrimination, resulting in the lack of minorities and women in positions of authority? Put them in positions of authority (affirmative action). Pollution? Regulate industry to impose limits (the regulatory state). In other words, direct government intervention to solve social ills. If society is economically unequal, then redistribute money from rich to poor through taxation and subsidies; if groups are discriminated against in hiring, housing, or public treatment, give them legal protections enforced by the government. The policy prescriptions are a straightforward set of redistributions and protections for the oppressed. How to improve society is not really a question, but is obvious. Once the oppressed and the source of oppression are identified, whether we can do anything about it is a conservative rather than liberal question. Without the premise of perfectionism, and with the premises of a negative human nature and social fragility, it becomes a difficult question of exactly how to alter existing conditions. It is not obvious that we can fix any of these problems; it is likely that our interventions could make them worse; and it is almost certain that we will cause other unforeseen problems in the effort. But with a different set of premises, it is not the method that is in question, but only the focus of our effort. Because bold experimentation is the standard, policies can always be adjusted in order to be more effective. The important thing is to try. The divisive point is what to try first. The real question about oppression is *who is most oppressed?*

In the beginning and middle of the twentieth century, the central source of oppression was clear and uncontroversial. According to the mainstream beliefs of that time, it was obviously economic. Class divisions and persistent poverty were the root of the limited opportunities, stunted futures, and wide disparities in social status and political influence that faced many Americans. The focus of Progressive era politics in the early 1900s and then Depression era politics of the 1930s was to open doors to citizens who began in poverty but had the ability to contribute much more to society than these constraints allowed. Limiting corporate monopolies to allow for greater competition from small businesses, increasing the power of labor unions to improve the standing of working men, broadening public education and enforcing child labor laws, offering unemployment insurance and other protections to aid families during hard times, implementing the G.I. Bill to allow working-class veterans to attend college—all of these improvements were intended to alter the prevailing norms and power structures that stratified our society into wealthy, middle, and poor depending on birth rather than merit.

In the early twenty-first century, the central source of oppression is no longer so clear. After the civil rights movement, the women's movement, and the gay rights movement, it is no longer class or economic equality that is foremost in many liberals' minds. We have moved from a concern from wealth and poverty to an emphasis on category inequality grounded in gender, race, sexual orientation, ethnicity, or immigrant status. In the social science literature this is referred to as the shift from redistribution to recognition, from income to identity. But was it a movement from one to the other, or simply the addition of a second set of concerns along with the earlier ones? At first this change may seem to be simply a broadening of the concept of oppression and therefore an increase in social justice. But it highlights two critical points: (1) we no longer agree at all about who is oppressed, or oppressed most, and (2) the different ideas compete for support and resources. Every ounce of public concern or pile of dollars that goes to one group does not go to another.

An example of this competition occurs over university admissions and aid. At elite and costly colleges, there are a limited number of positions and a limited number of dollars in financial aid that are awarded. We can pretend that the widening of concern for different categories of oppression also increases the aid available, but this is not really true. Colleges must decide what they will subsidize and who will get the available money. Will it go to poor kids, minority kids, international students, disabled students, or increasing the number of female athletes? The overall goal is described as diversity, but this is a blanket term for all of these distinctions and other ones, all of which stake a claim for priority. This is one of the reasons that universities make these decisions behind closed doors and do not discuss their methods publicly. To do so would reveal their choices and invite great public criticism by the groups who believed they had not gotten their fair share. A reasonable person might suggest that we should simply divide the pie equally among these groups, but that will satisfy few of them because of the oppression problem, or the perception that they are not all equally oppressed and different groups should have priority.

In the 2008 presidential primary campaign, Hillary Clinton argued that the largest impediment to achievement in America is gender. That might seem reasonable in the context of her campaign, but is it really true? Is gender the single largest source of oppression? If that is the case, we should alter our political concerns, legislative agenda, and funding of social programs in vital ways. If it is true. If being female holds people back more than being a minority. Or more than being a recent immigrant. Or more than being poor. There are hardcore supporters of Clinton's proposition. But there are also hardcore opponents, not because they believe that women face no obstacles, but because they believe that another group is oppressed *more*, and is more deserving of our attention. In my classes I often ask the question: if you were a 10-year-old American kid with a burning ambition to be something difficult to become, like a doctor (or maybe even with a less specific goal, like being an economically secure and productive member of society), would you be more likely to succeed if you were a girl from an affluent family, or a boy from a poor one? Answers differ, and how someone answers this question is telling. If we change the categories from gender and wealth to race, immigrant status, sexual orientation, etc., it becomes even more complex and debatable.

More than simply a zero-sum game in which political attention and resources that go to one concern do not go to another, there are further divisions between some groups. It is not merely a matter of resource competition but also ideological and moral disagreement. Not all members of the liberal coalition agree with the claims of other members. One historical division has been between blacks and Hispanics, both of whom claim status as the most disadvantaged participants in the job market. The rising numbers of Hispanic Americans, the increasing publicity to the conditions of migrant labor, and paradoxically the increasing success of African Americans at entering the professions, have altered the public perception of who has the obvious claim to needing assistance. A perhaps more serious division separates the claims of race and sexuality. One of the American demographic groups that is least accepting of claims of gay rights are African Americans. The argument that the gay rights movement is the same as the civil rights movement falls on deaf ears to many who participated in the civil rights protests, who do not believe that the discrimination against homosexuals compares to what was suffered historically by blacks. African Americans are also less likely than others to accept the view that homosexuality is innate rather than chosen behavior, perhaps because of the greater religiosity within the black community. In California in 2008, the same electorate that chose Barack Obama voted in favor of Proposition 8 limiting marriage to unions between a man and a woman. This surprised many liberals who assumed that it is natural to back both civil rights and gay rights. They did not foresee that the rising African American turnout in that election would not only advantage Obama but also the initiative against gay marriage.

The recent prominence of the gay marriage debate has shifted many Americans, especially younger ones, toward feeling that homosexuals are the more oppressed group. To older liberal thinkers, the idea that one of the most affluent and best-educated demographic groups, who tend to hold high status occupations, could be the most oppressed is ludicrous when compared to poor Americans. Yes, homosexuals can't legally marry, but poor people can't easily become educated, have a good job, enjoy quality health care, or have much professional prospect, which many might trade for not getting married legally. This highlights the distinct division between advocates of each of the more recent categories of concern compared to the older focus on economic oppression. Many traditional liberals believe that this should still be the primary focus. We did not win that battle and then move on to category inequality. We did not win yet, and the primary economic battle is still the most important one, cutting across concerns of race, ethnicity, and gender to go to the real issue that determines an American citizen's prospects: wealth or poverty. The oppression problem—or the problem of who is oppressed—is a source of great division.

9

LIBERALISM

Branches

Which form of oppression is most severe? Who is most deserving of our attention and aid? The prominent answers to this question explain the divisions within contemporary liberalism, competing for moral standing, political attention, and limited resources.

Class

Traditional liberals see the poor as the most oppressed group in America. The large and growing gap between wealthy and impoverished is the cen-

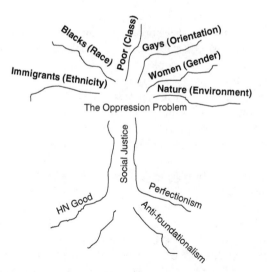

Figure 9.1 Liberal Branches

tral source of oppression. Three distinct aspects of economic differences create significant gaps in social justice. The first and most obvious is literal privation, or the grinding poverty that insures that most people caught within it will never advance. This includes an environment of social pathologies, from underperforming and unsafe schools, to the crime, drug abuse, and youth prostitution that derail so many young people before they have much of a chance at a decent life. Much of this has to do with access to quality education, at both lower and upper levels. One of the great sources of disparity in our system is that public schools are funded locally, which means that poor neighborhoods have poor schools. One can argue that some of the adults caught in poverty and degenerate living conditions brought it on themselves through bad choices, but it is hard to maintain that the kids growing up with those limitations did something to deserve it as well.

The second aspect of the oppression of class differences is the lack of opportunity created by entrenched privileges. Simply put, when the children of wealthy families have such clear advantages over other talented people, it leaves little opportunity for others to compete and rise. This problem has grown in recent decades along with the increasing disparity between the truly wealthy and middle America. While incomes in the middle have remained relatively stagnant in the last decades, income and collected wealth at the top has expanded tremendously. There are now simply far more families with substantial wealth, enough to sincerely influence the trajectory of their children. This is especially influential in an age when university tuition costs have risen at over twice the rate of inflation and priced elite education out of the range of normal people.[1]

In all of the professions and positions in our society that are limited in number, such as doctors, lawyers, professors, business executives, etc., the people who can command the resources that allow for private schooling, tutors, and excellent colleges will have tremendous advantages over everyone else. People who come from families with connections in the professions, universities, corporations, and government will find much easier pathways into those positions. The playing field may never be leveled, but the greater the differences between the wealthy and everyone else, the harder it is for normal people to achieve. This is not only a matter of equality, but also of efficiency. We want the most capable people to be doctors and engineers, or leaders in business, academics, and government, not merely the ones with greater access. We all pay a price when mediocrities from wealthy families take places that should have gone to more capable people from working-class backgrounds.

The least obvious aspect of class oppression may be the disparities in political power. Because political campaigns require substantial funding, influence within democratic politics is directly correlated with wealth. Affluent voices are heard, and truly wealthy voices speak very loudly, while the interests of the poor are often ignored or exploited.

The history of social advancements during the twentieth century is highlighted by efforts to allow all Americans a piece of the American Dream. The government programs of the New Deal, the Great Society, Social Security, the welfare safety net, unemployment payments, subsidies of higher education, and most recently national health care, are some of the efforts to decrease poverty and increase the opportunity of young people born without resources to nonetheless rise to their level of ability and take their place as influential citizens.

This view of what is at the heart of the issue, and which government actions represent the most important advances, is embraced by traditional liberals but disputed by others. Most importantly, multiculturalist liberals have a different perspective. *Multiculturalism* is a broad term that has been overused to describe many things, but it includes the rise of the view that racial, ethnic, and other category differences are the real source of discrimination and oppression. Its core argument is that all races, cultures, creeds, religions, ethnicities, sexual orientations, and other social differences should be embraced and respected within a mosaic of American citizens. Assimilation, nationalism, and traditional norms or roles should not limit any individual or be imposed on any group. This emphasis is quite different from the older concerns of economic inequality and class oppression, leading to a different set of priorities. The rise of multiculturalism led to a broad shift in liberal perspectives.

Race

Many liberals see minorities, especially African Americans, as the most oppressed group. Racism remains a powerful source of oppression. No other group in America has a comparable history of slavery, Jim Crow laws, and lingering resentments. This has created a distinct status for the descendants of slaves, which other Americans, new and old, do not face and have trouble even comprehending from the perspective of African Americans. Some argue that explicit racism has decline to negligible levels, but to many others it is clear that more subtle forms of racism and disproval still linger. Blacks remain more impoverished, more likely to go to jail, and less likely to finish high school, go to college, or hold a high-status job than whites.

The civil rights movement and the achievements of landmark legislation such as the Civil Rights Act of 1964 and the Voting Rights Act of 1965 have altered much of the landscape of race and inclusion across America. The policy focus with regard to race is now affirmative action in university admissions, hiring decisions by corporations and government agencies, and in awarding government contracts, all designed to overcome the combination of psychological blocks and entrenched disparities in education and status that limit the inclusion of blacks. Many advocates and scholars now refer to this not as racism, but "white privilege." This is a controversial idea, among liberals as well as conservatives. It suggests that all whites are privileged over all blacks. In this sense the overriding source of oppression in America is race, not wealth or economic status.

The dispute over this point was the centerpiece of a prominent editorial by Jim Webb, the Democratic senator from Virginia, who was widely discussed as a possible running mate for Barack Obama in 2008.[2] Webb points out some significant points: multicultural policies targeted toward all people of color have "lessened the focus on assisting African-Americans, who despite a veneer of successful people at the very top still experience high rates of poverty, drug abuse, incarceration and family breakup." But Webb's main point is that he opposes affirmative action policies because "contrary to assumptions in the law, white America is hardly a monolith." In his view it is a citizen's wealth and opportunity that holds them back or raises them up, not principally their skin color. All whites are not privileged, nor are all blacks lacking privilege, depending on their economic origins. The heart of the disagreement is which form of oppression trumps the other, and therefore which policies we should give priority and where we should expend resources.

Gender

From another perspective, women are the most oppressed group in America. The limits to advancement and equal treatment faced by half of America are the largest source of oppression. These same factors are also the largest source of oppression worldwide. The total loss in talent and productivity created by the exclusion of women is staggering. This perspective of course suggests different priorities in affirmative action policies, different emphases in educational policy, and a different conversation about which public and personal attitudes need to change in order to achieve social justice.

Sexual Orientation

From a more recent perspective, the tip of the sword in the battle against oppression is the gay rights movement. But many Americans who recognize the plight of the poor, the history of racism, or the pervasive gender distinctions in our society refuse to see gay rights and civil rights as comparable. Others see the denial of full standing of same-sex relationships as a fundamental source of oppression that should be addressed before other concerns. Especially since other groups have already benefited from social movements and government actions that have improved their standing dramatically, while homosexuals still inhabit a cultural ghetto of exclusion.

Ethnicity and Immigrant Status

Another group of liberals looks across the American landscape and sees the oppression of recent immigrants, especially Hispanics, as the most virulent kind. The increasing presence of Hispanic Americans has brought public resentment as well as official harassment in border states like Arizona. Aside from the organized attempts to exclude new Americans from participation in our society, the conditions of migrant laborers are some of the worst of any minority group in the nation. Hispanics and Latinos are around 15 percent of the total U.S. population, which surpassed the number of African Americans (at about 13 percent) sometime around 2002. The Census Bureau estimates that by 2050 the total number of Hispanics will be about 25 percent of the population (compared to blacks at 15 percent), due to high fertility and immigration rates. Hispanics are no longer willing to see themselves as the less important or deserving minority group.

Environmentalism

A final and growing argument is that the claims of the environment should trump other concerns. In this view the most oppressed entity is *nature* rather than any specific human group. We have a history of despoiling the environment, which has been somewhat controlled by the landmark clean air and water legislation, but there are many long-term problems yet to be solved. The early conservation movement grounded in preserving natural wonders and species evolved in the 1970s into the ecology movement focused on maintaining a sustainable balance in the natural ecosystem. This is not just a matter of human interest, but also the rights of non-human species. While some liberals dispute that animals have rights and argue that we should focus on our own living conditions, they do not deny that there is an element of human environmental justice that can't be ignored: the people most likely to live in areas with low air and water quality are the poor, and the areas most likely to have landfills and environmental contaminants are poor neighborhoods. The most pressing current concern is global warming and climate change, which demands the attention of the federal government and world bodies such as the UN before we pass the point of irrevocable damage to the planet. This concern is so potentially devastating that it trumps commitments of resources to other liberal causes.

The competition between environmental liberals and others is not just about moral standing and issue space. Environmental initiatives are often opposed by blue collar liberals, especially the labor unions that formed a traditional source of liberal support, because of the tension between economic development and job creation versus environmental controls. So far the promise of green jobs has not lived up to the pay and status of skilled labor jobs. Environmental programs such as cap and trade, emission limits, or especially plans to combat global climate change may seem like reasonable ideas that all liberals can support, until the price tags are clear and the necessary trade-offs with other spending become unavoidable.

So how do we weigh the competing claims of class, race, gender, sexual orientation, ethnicity, and the environment? Who is most oppressed, the poor, blacks, women, gays, immigrants, or nature? Who gets priority in our politics? These divisions often cause liberals to be more competitive than cooperative, even though their goal of equality and social justice is the same. The competing claims of class versus identity, gender versus race, race versus ethnicity, sexual orientation versus race and class, or the claims of nature versus the interests of various human groups all create a liberal dilemma. Martin Luther King was fond of quoting Theodore Parker, an influential Unitarian minister and abolitionist who died just before the outbreak of the Civil War. He said that, "the arc of the moral universe is long, but it bends toward justice." Movement toward social justice is the undisputed goal, but the question is where to head first?

Part III

COMPARISONS AND CONTROVERSIES

10

EMOTIONS AND NIGHTMARES

The descriptions of conservatism and liberalism in the earlier pages concentrate on the foundational premises and core values that characterize the two worldviews, as well as the central questions and competing answers that create the branches of each ideology. There are other renditions that also reveal important aspects of their perspectives. The ideologies could be described simply as clusters of competing values. This would be accurate, but incomplete. It does not explain *why* those values fit together. To see the coherence of each ideology, we need to see the underlying beliefs that determine other important value commitments. The ideologies could also be described as specific collections of policy preferences, but again we would be hard pressed to say how they fit together without recognizing the foundational beliefs. Nonetheless, those policy disagreements are important to understand, even though they are the result rather than the basis of the ideologies. This final set of short chapters discusses the two ideologies from the perspective of *contemporary value conflicts*, *divisive issues*, and also the *emotions* that shape each perspective. These chapters also examine important comparisons between the ideologies as well as central divisions within them, specifically the recent split among conservatives between *paleocons* and *neocons*, and the rise of *multiculturalism* as opposed to traditional liberalism.

Foundational perceptions of reality and core values drive the two ideologies, but certain underlying emotions also influence their arguments. Ideologies and political conflicts are not just about ideas, but also about deeper gut reactions. *Each ideology has a central emotion that lies at its core.* These can be described in positive terms or negative ones, depending on the spin one wants to offer. I prefer to use the negative words, because I believe they are more accurate and because they convey what is really motivating the worldview. Believers on each side will no doubt prefer the more favorable

71

description, but this book is not written to please them, but instead to make their worldviews understandable.

Another reason to see the underlying emotions from the less flattering perspective is that politics is driven by the negative more than the positive. Citizens engage in politics more often because of what they can't stand than because of what they would like to see; voters often choose *against* rather than vote *for*. This makes sense when we realize that the psychology of the negative is more powerful than the psychology of the positive. One of the central findings of cognitive psychology is that losses loom larger in the psyche than gains. We are more pained by losing something that we have than we are pleased by gaining something we want. This negativity bias applies strongly to political decision-making and engagement. Many people complain about negative ads during campaign season. Some argue that they alienate voters from our political system. So why are they so common? Because they work. Negative motivation beats positive motivation. Which explains why understanding the core emotions in their negative frame gives us more insight into the ideologies, especially conservatism.

The central emotion driving conservatism is fear. This could be described as prudence, but to be clear, it is fear of loss, fear of decline, and fear of violence. It is the gnawing knowledge of enemies, predators, and degenerates. This makes courage, patriotism, and sacrifice highly valued in conservative thought, because there are things to fear, and we must have people who can handle them.

Fear is the driving force of the glue problem. Society can decline and collapse. We can lose a great deal of what we love, including a free and decent society. Protecting this is the most important thing we can do, which demands prudent concern, or appropriate worry. To paraphrase Gordon Gekko in *Wall Street*, greed may not be good, but fear is. Fear is good because it keeps us alert.

The liberal emotion is quite different. *The central emotion driving liberalism is guilt.* This is often described in the positive sense as compassion or empathy. "I feel your pain" was a famous and effective line of Bill Clinton's. But the negative framing and more powerful driver is guilt. Sometimes it is guilt about our wealth and privilege compared to those without; sometimes it is guilt over the past treatment of minorities and their current lack of equal standing; sometimes it is guilt over the advantages of being male; or guilt over how America has dominated other nations; or guilt over how we have despoiled nature and continue to be responsible for the disruption of the climate. There are many facets of liberal guilt, but they all reduce to the same emotional core.

Guilt is the driving emotion of the oppression problem. Who is oppressed most? About whom are we most guilty? The answer depends on our own position and history. The group we personally feel more guilt about is not the same question as who is truly most disadvantaged. But the two questions can easily become conflated and confused.

No doubt both conservatives and liberals will disagree with these descriptions. It is not fear, but patriotism; it is not guilt, but compassion. I have no desire to quibble over these characterizations, but the point remains that powerful emotions—in their negative or positive frame—are at the heart of each ideology.

In addition to the role of conservative fear and liberal guilt, another way to gain insight into the ideologies is to identify their nightmare scenarios. What do they most want to avoid, but believe might happen if their approach is not followed? Earlier we identified the core conservative question: how can a world of liberty not be a world of license? The answers lead us to focus on *protecting* society. The liberal question is how can we make the world better by alleviating oppression? This leads us to focus on *perfecting* society. These ideas, combined with each ideology's core emotion, make the nightmare scenarios clear. For conservatives it is social collapse. The can result from internal decline, or from external enemies, or more likely from the first inviting the second, but the end is the same. Conservatives often cite a famous poem by William Butler Yeats that summarizes this fear:

> Turning and turning in the widening gyre
> The falcon cannot hear the falconer;
> Things fall apart; the centre cannot hold;
> Mere anarchy is loosed upon the world,
> The blood-dimmed tide is loosed, and everywhere
> The ceremony of innocence is drowned;
> The best lack all conviction, while the worst
> Are full of passionate intensity.[1]

Note the line, "Things fall apart," which has been quoted in many places, including the title of an important novel.[2] "The centre cannot hold" is a military reference to the center of the line collapsing under assault, but is also a nod to the golden mean philosophy of conservatism; the virtuous middle path is crushed by one of the two extremes. A part of Yeats' argument is that apathy and selfishness can lead to decline as quickly as the lack of national unity and encroaching enemies. If the best lack all conviction—if anything goes and nothing is believed without doubt—then we have lost.

But this is not the only conservative nightmare. Conservatism is grounded in the fear of anarchy on the one side, but also of tyranny on the other. The goal is to remain in the golden mean between those two extremes. The other nightmare is the death of liberty at the hands of organized government rather than disorganized barbarians. This is the dark vision of George Orwell's *1984*. In that classic dystopian novel, a collectivist government with a will to dominate for its own sake destroys the ability of individuals to have privacy, humor, decency, or even love. This is the extreme version of collectivism and statism that conservatives fear, beginning with lesser versions of government intervention into the private lives of citizens. To quote Stephen Colbert, of the Colbert Report, fake conservative talk show host and real liberal comedian, "America, the Greatest Country God ever gave Man, was built on three bedrock principles: Freedom, Liberty. And Fear—that someone might take our Freedom and Liberty."[3] Interestingly, the same thing that is a joke to liberals is a serious thing to conservatives.

The liberal nightmare scenario is quite different. It is the complete oppression of the weak by the privileged; the total dominance by the wealthy and elite over the poor, over minorities, over women, and over every other vulnerable group. This could only come to its full fruition if the privileged employed the coercive power of government to quash dissent and deprive individuals of free expression. This is not the collectivist tyranny of conservative worries, but a more fascist tyranny grounded in extreme nationalism and militarism, in which the state employs the police to entrench the power of an authoritarian elite. Every form of oppression that liberals want to erase would instead be increased. Homosexuals could be deprived of rights, and immigrants could be treated as second-class citizens. Nature would be despoiled without respite. Halting the advancement of any form of social justice is a setback, but erasing all of them simultaneously is the true nightmare, retreating into a world of baseless fear, restricted lives, social divisions, and needless war.

The question for each of the potential nightmare scenarios is what will our grandchildren's lives be like? Will your granddaughter be poor, unsafe, or oppressed? From the conservative perspective, she could be poor because of the rise of state socialism, or unsafe because of the growth of external enemies coupled with the fall of Western freedoms. From the liberal perspective, she could be poor because of the dominance of the wealthy, and oppressed because of government authoritarianism. These different concerns are at the root of the conflicting impulses of American citizens in response to terrorism in the post-9/11 world. Which scenario is more likely? (1) That we will lose our liberties through the destruction of our ability to travel or gather in groups because of terrorist bombings, and through restrictions on free expression because of fear of offending Muslims? Or (2) That we will lose our liberties because of government actions aimed at terrorists but having the effect of spying on Americans and inhibiting free expression? Will the losses of freedom be imposed by harsh reality and self-censorship, or by imperial government and authoritarian restrictions? The answer depends on our view of the competing likelihood of conservative and liberal nightmare scenarios.

But it would be misleading to say that liberals and conservatives are equally motivated by their nightmares. Because fear looms larger in the conservative mind, their nightmares play a larger role. This allows the power of negative motivations to work in their favor. The dual concerns of social collapse on one side and government tyranny on the other also provide more scope for worry. Conservatives simply have more, and more fearful, nightmares than liberals. This predicament is summarized well by the famous filmmaker Werner Herzog, probably best-known for *Aguirre: The Wrath of God*, *Nosferatu*, and *Grizzly Man*: "I try to understand the ocean beneath the thin layer of ice that is civilization. There is miles and miles of deep ocean, of darkness and barbarism. And I know the ice can break easily."

11

VALUE DIVIDES

Many observers believe that our political culture is increasingly divided. In the early 1990s scholars began speaking of a culture war that began in the 1970s and has been growing in strength since then. It divides our secular citizens against our religious, our urban versus rural. Our traditionalists uphold the older values of patriotism, nationalism, and nuclear families, while our progressives promote the acceptance of new social arrangements and the freedom to choose among them. This creates another way of understanding the competing ideologies, which take clear positions between Red and Blue America, between our traditionalist and progressive values. James Hunter's book *Culture Wars* popularized the term, which is employed frequently by political pundits and media commentators.[1] "Red states"—the more religious and rural states of the South and Midwest—are contrasted with the "blue states" of the more secular and urban Northeast and West Coast. While the coastal states and flyover states have distinct cultures, the greater political differences are between the urban and rural areas *within* those states. For example, Pennsylvania is neither a red or blue state, nor a purple state as it is sometimes described. It is strongly blue in the major cities, and clearly red in the rest of the state. Having grown up in central PA and spent many years in Pittsburgh, I am familiar with the saying that Pennsylvania is Philadelphia and Pittsburgh separated by Alabama.

It has become harder to argue that our politics and society are unified around common values. We increasingly live in one of two worlds, which have different perceptions, different jokes, different heroes, and different sources of information. We less frequently have friends across the divide, and find it harder to talk to people from the other culture without causing misunderstandings or giving offense. The root of the division is sometimes described as the growing differences in wealth, but red America encompasses both poor and wealthy. The old assumptions that the more money someone has the less they are in favor of redistributing wealth, and the more poor they are the more they favor government intervention is no longer true. Wealthy liberals and working-class conservatives are now normal. It is less the distinction between the "haves and have nots" that divides our politics, and more the attitudes toward having. Many of our poor accept the legitimacy of accumulating wealth, and many of our wealthy feel guilty about theirs. It may be more accurate to describe the cultural divide as grounded in competing core values.

We can identify at least four major value clashes that form the core of our current politics. The strongest division may be between *religiosity* and *secularism*. Many scholars predicted in the 1960s and 1970s that America would become increasingly secular as faith in God and organized religion faded. They were right about part of that, as the number of secular Americans has grown. More citizens than ever before profess no belief in God. But the number of devout has also grown. We are witnessing a broad and unpredicted expansion in religious faith across several fronts. The Catholic Church is expanding, and the Mormon faith is growing even more rapidly, spreading way beyond the confines of Utah and into the ranks of influential public figures such as Mitt Romney and Glenn Beck. The most significant change politically has been the rise of Evangelical Protestantism as a social force and strong influence within the Republican Party. We have not witnessed merely the rise of secularism or of religiosity, but of both. The middle has shrunk, and the numbers of both truly secular and truly religious have grown, dividing our public culture and our interpretation of political events. This value dimension may be one of the most influential because it is clear, attached to strong emotions, and has ramifications that are easy to understand. It is an umbrella for a large number of political positions that have moral dimensions.

Another clear divide is between an *individual* or a *community* orientation. On the one side, many Americans have a strong inclination toward personal responsibility and individual decision-making. More than most Western nations, we respect and admire the role of the individual. But the American frontier experience was not only about rugged individualism. It also required group efforts and mutual protection in order to survive and thrive. Not only did the individual have duties to the group, but the group took responsibility for the weaker members. Our communitarian perspective stresses the claims that individuals can legitimately make for help from the rest of us, especially in hard times. This value divide influences our political debate across a wide range of issues regarding economic redistribution, government regulation, health care, taxation, and the welfare state.

The divisions in our domestic politics—between individualists versus communitarians, and religious versus seculars—are matched by a deep divide in foreign affairs. More *militarist* versus more *pacifist* values explain a great deal about our reactions to world events, especially the Middle Eastern wars. Militarism suggests an acceptance of the need for force in dealing with other countries, and the use of our military to protect ourselves and defend our interests. It leads to support for large defense budgets, and a gut reaction that if we are threatened we should respond in kind. It also entails a respect for the military and an emotional identification with military service and its symbols. More pacifist values lead to the opposite reaction when we are faced with discord with other nations or threats toward our allies. This orientation suggests a deep suspicion that militarism begets militarism, and that the use of force is likely to make a situation worse rather than better. We should emphasize negotiation and the search for compromise whenever possible before taking military action.

This value division is connected to feelings of *nationalism* versus *internationalism*, a related but somewhat distinct value dimension. Nationalists are more attached to an American identity and see it as natural to think in terms of our national interest, or a clear division between *us* and *them*. Internationalists, on the other hand, see all human interests as roughly equal and resist pursuing a purely American perspective as our natural goal. They see themselves more as citizens of the world than purely American partisans. Even citizens with clear leanings toward one value over the other may object to the terms used here to describe them. "Militarism" sounds too harsh and "pacifism" sounds too weak, while "internationalists" have not lost all identification with America and "nationalists" do no lack any concern for other people. But the labels make the point clear about who leans in which direction, even if not to the full extreme. Because we live in an era of warfighting—in Afghanistan and Iraq, as well as against Islamist terror groups—the value clashes between militarism and pacifism, as well as nationalism and internationalism, have become more influential and divisive.

A final value that is increasingly controversial can be summarized as a regard for traditional social arrangements—marriage, family, gender roles, and strong parenting—versus an openness to new ways of choosing to live. Whether it is gay marriages, single mothers, stay at home dads, or other choices, the liberal position is that individuals should be free to build their own existences without interference or social stigma. Conservatives advocate the public respect and regard for traditional institutions in order to maintain a strong society that supports the needs of the next generation.

This value clash between *tradition* and *openness* applies to several of the most divisive debates in our current culture.

Conservatives strongly support individualism, religiosity, militarism, and tradition; liberals clearly support the opposite values of communitarianism, secularism, pacifism, and openness. This alone provides a working description of the two ideologies. But it does not explain *why* those values group together as they do. In the tree diagram conception of ideology, the values of each worldview form the trunk of the tree. The conservative value of ordered liberty leading to individual dignity, and the liberal value of social justice leading to greater equality, form the core of the trunk. These core values and the premises at their roots explain the conservative and liberal positions on the other value divisions.

In regard to individual versus community orientations, conservatives make a claim for the individual. Personal responsibility is a clear value, as is individual decision-making. This leads conservatives to uphold property rights and worry that government intervention will be unproductive at the same time that it lessens liberty. Many conservatives are quite charitable (in fact, conservatives of any given income consistently give more money to charities than liberals in the same income range), but this is a matter of personal choice rather than government mandate, flowing to private institutions, especially churches, rather than government programs. The observation that individualists give more money to charities than communitarians seems odd until you see how it fits with the belief systems. Conservatives actually believe that charity is a private function that the government should not be doing, and individuals should be. Liberals, on the other hand, are committed to a leading government role in social welfare and would vote for increased taxes to pay for this. But they do not believe it is as much a matter of personal action and choice, which explains their giving patterns.

The conservative attachment to individualism stems directly from the commitment to ordered liberty. There are legitimate limits to individual liberty, but only those that protect a decent world and maintain social order. Other attempts to change society merely degrade liberty with little payoff. In this view, individual dignity trumps collective purposes, even possibly beneficial ones. The premises of conservatism also reinforce this value. If society is fragile, then we must maximize our total economic production for our national strength, rather than make tradeoffs for greater equality. Property rights and their incentives provide not only economic efficiency, but also the kind of social order that is necessary to stabilize the community. Because human nature cannot be trusted, property must be protected against the depredations of others, whether criminals or government. The anti-utopian premise also reinforces the idea that communitarian schemes fail because they go against the essential nature of man.

But the liberal set of premises and values lead to exactly the opposite conclusion. The potential for perfectibility suggests that communitarian efforts will bear fruit. The improvement of society is not an individual task, but a group effort that requires collective decision-making and commitment. A positive view of human nature suggests that individuals will live up to those commitments and fulfill their responsibilities to weaker members of our enterprise. But it is the goal of social justice that makes a group orientation most clear. The community must make a place for all of its people, and enforce norms that protect weaker members. Social justice for oppressed groups can only occur when there is a social commitment to act in their interests. This means that cooperation trumps competition, and group solutions are more important than individual interests.

The differences between liberals and conservatives are also tied to competing perceptions of the basic unit of society, which could be the individual, or it might be the family, or it could be social groups (grounded in ethnicity, occupation, culture, religion, etc.), or it could be society as a whole. The question is how we think of ourselves, and how we believe we should be organized. The disagreement is illustrated by two competing quotes during the 2008 campaign season. Hillary Clinton was fond of saying, "It takes a village," while Charlton Heston, former NRA president and conservative activist, shot back, "It takes a family." Which of these visions represents the best society is a source of great disagreement.

Figure 11.1 illustrates the ideological divisions over the basic unit of society. Our politics often focus on responsibilities, or the question of who has duties to others. Is it individuals who are responsible for themselves, or society that is responsible for the welfare of individuals? Conservatives clearly believe that the source of legitimate responsibility is individuals and their families. We have strong duties to take care of ourselves and support our own families, but not necessarily toward others. Liberals see a strong responsibility of the community to take care of its members, which means that individuals must contribute to the group in the form of taxes. The vision of a society organized by individuals and families creates a very different set of commitments than a society grounded in group identifications. Whether it is a village or a family is no small distinction when it comes to many questions of welfare state programs and public values.

However, it is important to note that if we apply this interpretation of the basic unit of society as a broad generalization it begins to appear incorrect.

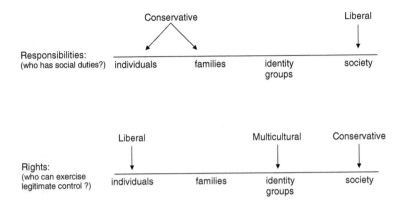

Figure 11.1 The Basic Unit of Society

In the realm of rights, or the question of who can legitimately control others, liberals and conservatives reverse positions. Liberals believe that individuals are the primary holders of rights, which means that civil liberties such as free speech, religious practice, or sexual conduct must not be infringed upon except under the most compelling circumstances. Conservatives believe that society as a whole has rights that enable us to maintain a decent environment. In the foreign policy realm, the ideological focus on the basic unit of society also reverses. When facing other nations, conservatives believe we should see ourselves as a unified whole. The most important social unit is the entire society, while liberals have less of a nationalistic leaning.

When it comes to the religious–secular divide, the commitment to social justice makes liberals wary of religious sentiment. Traditional religious doctrines and the judgmental nature of Christianity sound like oppression. Traditional Judeo-Christian attitudes toward homosexuality and in regard to the role of women also seem to limit more than liberate historically oppressed groups. If individuals are to have a free choice of lifestyles, then we must maintain a strict separation of church and state. Individual faith is one thing, but when it enters the public square it begins to oppress. The anti-foundationalist core of liberalism also rejects the faith and certain knowledge of the devout. We cannot know such things as certainties, and therefore certainly shouldn't push them on others. Conservatives tend to take the opposite view, embracing the stabilizing role of religious institutions because they fear social instability. Moral teachings are a bulwark against the negative view of human nature that is shared by conservatives and many branches of Christianity. Of the possible binding agents of a fragile society, religious tradition is one of the strongest contenders. It is also important to keep in mind that many conservatives did not gain that ideology first, and then were influenced to be religious. They were religious first, which is why they gravitated to conservatism. Religion leads to social conservatism more often than the reverse.

The same views on human nature and social fragility lead conservatives to embrace militarism and nationalism. A fragile society beset with enemies and permanently in a world of aggressive humans requires a strong defense. Utopian visions or attempts at world government will not replace the need for a warrior class. We will always need soldiers of the state, and they will always need the respect of the populace. The tradition and sacrifice of the armed services is honored in conservative families, who often have active and former soldiers. If we hold the opposite view of human nature, and believe that human societies have the potential to elevate themselves above violent conflict, then a militarist posture seems more counter-productive than necessary. Liberal premises about humans and society make a more pacifist and internationalist approach the natural position. The hierarchy and strict codes of the military seem like another form of oppression, which is increasingly archaic in the modern world. Greater admiration is reserved for other forms of community service and other forms of sacrifice.

When it comes to the division over traditional versus new social arrangements, the premise of anti-foundationalism plays a leading role in shaping the liberal value of openness. If we cannot have an absolute source of authoritative knowledge, or a bedrock set of unquestionable values, then we have no place dictating which ways of life are best. What we have done in the past is not a sufficient reason to insist that we continue it now. The core commitment to equality and social justice means that all groups and all ways of being must be accorded a respected position in society. All citizens should be able to get married as they choose, or live in the kind of household they prefer, without the interference of the state or the disapproval of society. The conservative view of new social arrangements stems from the same premises that drive their individualist and militarist values: social fragility and the problematic nature of humans. Traditional relationships bind society together and provide for the stability necessary to nurture a new generation. Gender roles and expectations offer a basis from which to build a decent society. If the world were not fragile and harsh, it might be different, but in the world as it is, traditional families are the source of our protection and humanity.

Our divisions along these value dimensions are entrenched and influential. Our political conflicts and public debates are shaped by them perhaps more than by any other influence. And the relation between ideology and these values is determined by the underlying beliefs that are at the heart of each worldview.

12

LIBERTY AND EQUALITY
Consensus Values with Conflictual Meanings

Americans have often been described as a pragmatic people. It is the results that count, and practical approaches to reach them that are admired. American politics can be described as *a pragmatic attempt to achieve our desired and feared principles*. Chief among these are liberty and equality. We desire liberty. Yet we fear it. We desire equality. But we fear it as well. The balance of desire and fear at any given time drives our political conflicts and also distinguishes conservatism from liberalism.

Each ideological worldview desires as well as fears our core values, but with different proportions of the two emotions. To conservatives, liberty is desired and feared equally. They seek a golden mean between the desire for freedom and the fear of anarchy, which is the central dilemma of the belief system. In regard to equality, there is more fear than desire. Too much equality strips the individual of dignity, replacing earned status and achievement with a false equalization. To liberals, both liberty and equality are desired more than feared. Because human nature is good, we do not need to fear individual liberty. It is only economic freedom, especially when taken to extremes of greed by corporations, that we need to fear when it leads to oppression. Equality is desired most, and feared very little. It is worth noting that fear is the stronger motivator for conservatives in regard to both values, which fits with the powerful role of that emotion in the conservative mind.

But different emotions are not the only things at play in the ideological reactions to liberty and equality. There are also differing definitions. So far we have emphasized the conflicts among American citizens, but several of our core values we hold in common. Among the consensus values of American politics, liberty and equality stand out as core commitments. But the definition of each value has evolved over the course of our history, such that the two ideologies both claim to uphold these principles but nonetheless strongly disagree on public policy. Liberty and equality are *consensus values with conflictual meanings*, creating one of the core distinctions between contemporary liberals and conservatives. Liberals cleave to the new definition of each value, while conservatives hold to the older definition. Their understandings of these concepts differ, even while their words are often the same.

Along with the major value clashes described above, the differences over liberty and equality also define the two ideologies. But the divisions are not as clear as they are over individualism versus communitarianism, or militarism versus pacifism. Both ideologies claim to defend liberty. Both claim to support equality. But they think of the two values in distinct ways that lead to misunderstandings and accusations of falsehoods. When conservatives plainly say that they are in favor of liberty, this often raises hackles among liberals, who believe that social conservatives in particular are intent on *limiting* personal liberty. The conflict lies in the definition of liberty, which is a central reason our citizens talk past each other, because they are defining the same words differently.

Old Liberty Versus New Liberty

At the time of the Founding, liberty was the core concern of the revolutionary generation. As a free people comprised of free men, they saw the dominance of an outside force—the British—as illegitimate and a violation of their basic rights. But this was not true until they had been forged into a separate community. The colonists originally saw themselves as displaced British, but through the tribulations of the New World and their collective experience fighting together in the French and Indian Wars (what the British called the Seven Years War), they came to have a separate identity. But this was a collective identity, the We the People of the Constitution, and their freedom was a collective one. They were able to decide their own path, to rule themselves free from interference from the British or anyone else. This was a majoritarian freedom rather than an individual one. The critical juxtaposition was the people versus outsiders, making us collectively or politically free.

In the century that followed, the American conception of liberty evolved in an individual direction. We continued to agree that we were a free people, able to run our own show against the intervention of others. But we also came to believe that individual rights were powerful and expansive. The crucial juxtaposition in this view is the individual versus the government, rather than the earlier view of the collective (represented through elective government) versus outside interference. This shift is reflected in the change in our view of the Bill of Rights. The First Amendment provisions of free speech, petition, assembly, and religion were originally conceived as majoritarian doctrines, which were limitations only on the national but not state or local governments, which could do as their majorities wished. These rights were re-interpreted in the twentieth century as individual freedoms that applied to all forms of government control.

We also emerged in our more recent history as a single national identity rather than a collection of more powerful local and group identities. The great turning point was the Civil War. Both in our use of language and our sense of belonging, we moved from a local to a national attachment. Before the Civil War, the United States *were*, afterward the United States *was*. The shift in thinking is apparent in one of our most abiding definitions of freedom, John Stuart Mill's *On Liberty*, which defines liberty as the right to do as one wishes until it causes literal harm to someone else. It is important to remember that this was a nineteenth-century evolution (published in 1859), which seems natural to us in the twenty-first century but was quite new at that time and would have seemed almost bizarre to most Americans in the early days of the nation. And even now, its doctrine of expansive individual freedom limited only by direct harm to others is *not* our controlling principle, specifically because it conflicts with our earlier and still prevalent notion of majoritarian liberty. The older view of freedom is grounded in ordered liberty rather than Mill's pure liberty. While liberals tend to accept the newer argument that only direct harm is a violation of other's rights, conservatives still believe that indirect harms must be taken seriously. Therefore, the majority can impose limits on individual actions in the name of decency, and encourage individual citizens to live up to their duties. To put it simply, *conservatives believe in indirect harms and majority rights; liberals do not*. The two American views now reside in an uneasy relationship. The individual liberty that is in ascension is embarrassed of its collective origins and would prefer to forget the majoritarian liberty that came first, but the earlier interpretation still makes powerful claims within our belief system.

Contemporary conservatives still value the older kind of liberty, a majority rather than individual right, which explains several of their policy preferences. Contemporary liberals value the newer conception of liberty, grounded in individual freedoms rather than majoritarian ones, which explains many of their own preferences. To be clear, it is not a matter of each side entirely rejecting the other's interpretation of liberty, but a question of which is privileged when the two come into conflict. Will majoritarian liberties trump individual ones or the reverse? This contest is at the heart of the contemporary debate on the status of same-sex marriage. From the perspective of the more modern conception of liberty, each individual has the right to live their life as they choose, with full access to all of the institutions of our society. To say that someone cannot marry as they would prefer is to violate their *individual* right of liberty. But to say that we as a society cannot set our own standard of conduct and chart our own future is to violate our *collective* right of liberty. The majoritarian right is the liberty of a free people to decide their own destiny, which brings into question exactly which people we have in mind.

Majoritarian liberty is connected to *federalism*, or the position that individual states or local governments should be able to set their own paths rather than be subservient to a national standard. In this view, neither Georgia nor Massachusetts is obliged to conform to a national norm. In a continental nation of diverse regions, we can simply be different. In the older view of liberty, the people of Utah can run their own show, free from dominance by New Englanders. If the people of Texas decide to have a different standard than the people of California, their freedom should not be limited. This is the foundation of federalism, and explains the conservative attachment to this principle. Individual states have a claim to their own freedom. Liberals, on the other hand, tend to oppose federalism in favor of a single national standard. Their primary concern is liberty from an individual rather than collective perspective, which is protected best by national rules grounded in personal rights that follow individuals wherever in the Union they may go. In this view, regional differences are not more important than individual rights. At heart, disagreements over same-sex marriage, as well as interpretations of federalism, are grounded in the two different conceptions of American freedom.

Old Equality Versus New Equality

The second core principle of our consensus values evolved in a similar fashion. Again there was an earlier conception of equality; again there was the emergence of a more contemporary interpretation; and again both views

Table 12.1 Old and New Definitions of Consensus Values

	Old	*New*
Freedom	Free society (ordered liberty)	Free individuals (pure liberty)
Equality	Legal equality	Economic equality

remain within our belief systems. Liberals privilege one view and conservatives the other, leading to incompatible positions that are both grounded in claims to support the same value.

Equality was originally framed as equality under law. Legal equality means that all citizens must face the same law with the same rules. This is the reason for the explicit constitutional prohibition against titles of nobility in America: in old Europe some people were by definition better than others, while here everyone must be seen as the same. This does not mean that individuals will not have great differences in wealth, achievement, position, or influence, but it does mean that the lowest and the highest will be treated the same by the government and the courts, just as they are accorded equal moral standing by other citizens.

Beginning in the late 1800s, a new concern emerged: equality of outcome. This was connected to several shifts in our history, including the rise of socialism as a powerful doctrine, the growth of communitarian social movements, the politics of the Progressive era at the beginning of twentieth century, and the New Deal following the Great Depression of the 1930s. In the newer view, legal equality alone is not sufficient when it results in great inequalities of wealth, power, or opportunity. This change in focus gave rise to one of the dominant concerns of twentieth-century American politics: taxation and redistribution, or the degree to which we would build the modern welfare state. In the last part of the century, the concern with purely economic equality gave way to the emphasis on gender and racial equality, followed by the current debates about gay rights. Conservatives continue to assert that equality under law is the best foundation, which creates equality of opportunity but not outcome, while liberals argue that equality under law is not enough, especially if entrenched privileges ensure that the result is gravely unequal outcomes and a lack of true opportunity.

The movement from economic equality to a focus on category equality is clear in the current debates about same-sex marriage, an issue that demonstrates the differing conceptions of equality for liberals and conservatives. Under our traditional definitions of marriage as a legal institution, homosexuals are equal under the law, which is to say that a gay man can marry a woman if he wants to; he is not excluded from the institution or treated differently than anyone else. This meets all of the requirements of equality under law. To ask for a separate institution (gay marriage) to be added is to seek special status, or more than equal treatment. But from the newer perspective on equality, grounded in outcome instead of standing, homosexuals do not end up in the same position as those able to marry and enjoy the benefits. They are excluded de facto, which means that gay couples do not have the ability to be equally unhappy in marriage as straight people. A similar difference is apparent in the debates surrounding affirmative action policies, especially in admission to universities, hiring of professionals, or promotion to positions of authority. Liberals argue that the only way to achieve any equality of outcome is to take gender and race (and increasing sexual orientation) into consideration, given the limits of economic and social exclusion that these groups face. Conservatives argue that this is a direct violation of equal treatment, as members of specific demographic groups are given preference, while those from another group (white males) are treated unequally. The important point is that both sides argue in favor of equality, but with different understandings of what that value means and requires, whether it is equality of outcome or equality under law.

While contemporary liberals and conservatives often speak the same language, they define the terms differently. Their conflicting understandings of liberty and equality ensure a continuing conflict over public policies, even while their unity of values ensures that these two principles will continue to be a bedrock of our political debate.

13

ISSUE POSITIONS AND MUTUAL MISUNDERSTANDINGS
Explaining Conservative and Liberal Policies

American ideology is often described as merely a collection of policy preferences, liberals lining up on the left side of each issue and conservatives on the right. In this view, a liberal is someone who supports legal abortion, affirmative action, environmental protection, gay marriage, gun control, inheritance taxes, national health care, and spending on the welfare state, while opposing military actions. Conservatives are the reverse. This is accurate, but does nothing to explain why this is the case, or why those issue positions go together. It is much more accurate to say that ideology is a set of beliefs that lead to those positions, rather than simply liberalism or conservatism being a collection of policy preferences. It is important to see the connection between the belief systems that we have discussed and the major political issues of the current day. This chapter illustrates in a brief fashion how the premises and values of the ideologies lead to these issue positions, and perhaps as importantly, how these same beliefs lead each side to misunderstand why the other takes the positions they do.

The underlying beliefs that we have considered so far are summarized in Table 13.1. With these beliefs in mind, we can see the roots of each distinct policy position. Table 13.2 represents a summary of the major political issues of our time. For each issue, the table identifies the most important ideological beliefs that shape the issue position, in order of premises, core values, current conflictual values, and emotions.

It is important to note that the pro and con designations in the table are general statements of the comparative positions of the ideologies rather than fully accurate descriptions. For example, liberals are not *in favor* of deficit spending as a goal, but are merely willing to allow it in order to pursue other goals, and conservatives are not *opposed* to the environment as much as they

90

Table 13.1 Underlying Beliefs of Liberalism and Conservatism

	Conservative	*Liberal*
Premises	Fragility Negative human nature Anti-utopianism	Perfectionism Positive human nature Anti-foundationalism
Core Values	Ordered liberty (freedom with decency)	Social justice (equality, tolerance)
Current Conflictual Values	Individualism Religiosity Militarism Nationalism Tradition	Communitarianism Secularism Pacifism Internationalism Openness
Emotions	Fear (caution)	Guilt (compassion)

Table 13.2 The Ideological Basis of Major Political Issues

Issue	*Conservative*	*Liberal*	*Basis*
Abortion	Con		religiosity, tradition
		Pro	anti-foundationalism, secularism, openness
Affirmative Action	Con		liberty, individualism
		Pro	perfectionism, social justice, equality, communitarianism, guilt
Deficit Spending	Con		anti-utopianism, fragility, fear
		Pro	perfectionism, social justice, communitarianism
Environment	Con		anti-utopianism
		Pro	perfectionism, social justice, communitarianism, guilt
Gay Marriage	Con		fragility, tradition, religiosity
		Pro	anti-foundationalism, social justice, equality, openness, secularism
Gun rights	Pro		HN bad, fragility, ordered liberty, individualism, fear
		Con	HN good, perfectionism, communitarianism
Illegal Immigration	Con		fragility, ordered liberty, nationalism, fear
		Pro	HN good, social justice, equality, internationalism, guilt

Table 13.2 Continued

Inheritance Taxes	Con		anti-utopianism, liberty, individualism
		Pro	perfectionism, equality, communitarianism
National Health Care	Con		fragility, anti-utopianism, individualism, fear
		Pro	perfectionism, social justice, communitarianism, compassion
Terrorism (Aggressive Response To)	Pro		fragility, HN bad, ordered liberty, militarism, nationalism, fear
		Con	HN good, pacifism
War (Afghan and Iraq)	Pro		fragility, HN bad, liberty, militarism, fear
		Con	social justice, pacifism
Welfare State Spending	Con		anti-utopianism, ordered liberty, individualism
		Pro	social justice, equality, communitarianism

simply do not want to pay for its protection given other more pressing spending priorities. Nor are liberals explicitly in favor of illegal immigration, but they are not adamantly opposed, as conservatives are. This particular issue serves as a clear example of the underlying beliefs that are driving the ideological positions. The conservative reaction to illegal immigration is driven by the fragility premise. Our society is susceptible to the disorder, disruption, and cultural change that broad illegal immigration is causing, especially in the border zones. Illegal immigration brings the threat of greater crime and poverty. The cultural ideas that Mexicans bring are not grounded in our traditional Anglo-Protestant belief system that includes perceptions of God-given rights and a strong work ethic for its own sake. Perhaps the greatest threat is the disintegration of a national language, leading to discord and decline, much like the cultural and political divide in Canada. The core value of ordered liberty dictates that we must have laws and maintain an orderly system of who is admitted as citizens, rather than blink at massive illegal and uncontrolled activity. The value of nationalism is also at play, in maintaining national borders and especially an American identity. Overarching all of these concerns is the emotion of fear—of disorder, of crime, of decline, of division. Because these elements of the conservative worldview intertwine in a powerful way, the position on illegal immigration is clear.

On the liberal side, the reaction is equally clear, but for entirely different reasons. Liberals are simply not as worried about possible negative consequences, and see the oppression of immigrants as wrong and offensive. Without the fragility premise, the concerns about cultural change or rising crime are simply not compelling. Moreover, they are clearly overridden by other commitments. The premise of a positive and malleable human nature means that we do not need to fear poor Mexicans any more than anyone else. They will adapt and assimilate just as previous waves of immigrants have. The core value of social justice and equality dictates that immigrants be treated with the same dignity and be accorded the same rights as everyone else. Yet migrant workers are some of the most powerless people in America. They are in the running for having the least rights, the least recourse to the law, the least political influence, and the least opportunity for advancement. The internationalist value of liberalism also shapes attitudes toward immigration. We should think of others are equally worthy as Americans, without the prejudice of nationalism. Excluding others from what we enjoy simply due to birth is at least objectionable if not oppressive. The driving emotion of guilt or compassion over the conditions of migrant laborers, who are the source of cheap fruit and vegetables for our own tables, also makes the appropriate position clear.

The issue of illegal immigration is interesting because of the balance of conservative and liberal beliefs that guide the policy views. Both camps have clear and understandable reasons for backing or resisting policies like building the border fence, deporting illegal aliens upon detection, or empowering police to ask for identification of citizenship. Depending on the underlying premises and values, these policies are normal prudence or oppressive harassment. The issues that are perhaps more interesting are those with an unbalanced set of underlying motivations. On these issues, instead of four or five elements of belief shaping the policy views for each side, there are a dominant group of ideas on one side. For these issues, one ideological view may be stronger and clearer than the other. The unbalanced issues include terrorism and gun rights on the right (six underlying beliefs to two, and five to three in Table 13.2), and the environment (four to one) and affirmative action (five to two) on the left. This may explain the more powerful belief and often political achievement of one side over the other on these issues.

By the same token that not all issues are motivated by the same number of underlying beliefs, not all beliefs are equally influential. Some elements of belief are found in the table more frequently as drivers of current issue positions. For liberals, the most prevalent beliefs accounting for the dozen political issues in the table are *social justice* at eight examples and *communitarianism* at seven, with *perfectionism* at six. The most common beliefs explaining conservative positions are *fragility* and *ordered liberty* at seven each, followed by *fear* with six, and *anti-utopianism* and *individualism* with five each.

A consistent theme across the policy divides is that liberals do not perceive the same threats that conservatives do. If these threats are not present, then we can receive the benefits of government policies without the worries. Conservatives worry that the chickens will come home to roost. This is true of several divisive issues, including welfare state spending, national health care, immigration, affirmative action, and reactions to terrorism. To conservatives, welfare robs individuals of dignity and creates dependency on the state. Taxation is theft at worst and at best a necessary evil whose distortions of the economy must be limited, while to liberals it is paying for important benefits and values, or as Oliver Wendell Holmes Jr. reportedly said, "taxes are the price we pay for a civilized society." To conservatives, the price is much higher than its total of dollars. On the issue of terrorism, policies of domestic surveillance, heightened security, and increased attention to young Muslim men are necessary steps to conservatives, but to liberals they are not useful and are oppressive to minorities. Because liberals do not perceive the possibilities for negative ramifications of their policies, conservatives generally think of liberals as foolish. This perception masks for conservatives what liberals really are, which is hopeful, or what can be described as risk-taking for a greater good. They are simply willing to try for a better world, regardless of potential backlashes, which they see as temporary, while successful improvements are permanent.

Because liberals do not perceive the same threats, they also tend to not believe conservatives who discuss them. From the liberal perspective, it seems more likely that conservatives are simply in favor of oppression rather than truly fearful of negative consequences. To liberals, the conservative fears seem so remote it is hard to believe that their opponents are being genuine. Instead they are simply bad people, with negative and selfish designs. Without understanding the ideologies clearly, it is easy to misconstrue their motives.

The previous chapter spoke of the conflicting definitions of liberty and equality. These are not the only important concepts that have competing definitions, leading to mutual misunderstanding. Another is the nature of government action in the two worldviews. When liberals hear conservatives speak of individual responsibility toward society, and collective rights to discourage egregious behavior, they hear an incitement to state oppression. This is simply the government telling people what to do in regard to personal moral decisions. But conservatives believe that people should do these things themselves; self-restraint is at the core of conservatism.

Government would not have to act if individuals took responsibility to constrain themselves. Our leaders should first exhort citizens to change their attitudes. When it does act, government is only authorized to reinforce social order, but not to seek social utopia. Conservatives specifically reject government action across a large realm. It is personal and public attitudes that count. The answer is a renewal of values, not government action. To liberals this sounds like no policy at all. The way to improve society is through direct government action; other things are simply not an answer. Government should act to lessen oppression and improve society, but morals are outside of that concern.

As I wrote this in August of 2010, one of the recent political events of note was the rally sponsored by Glenn Beck at the Lincoln Memorial. Beck, who was a well-known conservative commentator on FOX News, spoke mostly of religious values and a personal sense of patriotism to a crowd estimated from between 200,000 and a half a million people, one of the largest gatherings at a political rally in recent history. The following day on *Meet the Press*, the Democratic senator from Louisiana (Mary Landrieu) said, "What Glenn Beck misses is that it's not just talking, it's actually actions" that count. By this she meant *government* action, or "using the power of government in a positive way ... to do right by the people." To Landrieu and other liberals, what Beck had to say about personal values was not relevant, because government action is the focus of social improvement. To Beck, and other conservatives, government action offers nothing toward what counts most, which is the renewal of the crucial beliefs, both private and public, which create a good society.

Another important core concept that the two ideologies define very differently is oppression. To liberals, oppression is the cause of systematic differences between social groups. Differences in outcome between rich and poor, male and female, black and white are due to oppression, or socially enforced blocks to achievement and status, which are not the fault of individuals. To conservatives, not all differences in outcome are due to oppression, which only results from direct human actions that hold down the advancement of others, such as discrimination in job hiring. Naturally occurring conditions that are not intentionally enforced cannot be oppression. This difference in definition leads to several questions that we cannot answer with certainty. For example, are gender roles oppressive or natural? Conservatives tend to see enduring gender differences as a natural situation that cannot be considered oppression. The condition that men and women are different is not oppression, but nature. Only conditions created by us, and amenable to alteration by us, can be thought of as oppressive. Liberals understand these

95

relationships differently. Many conditions are created by us collectively. They are socially constructed and held in place by the efforts of some groups, even if they do not realize it. Gender is constructed and changeable, even if sex differences are not. Similar questions apply to racial relations in regard to whether historical oppression counts as contemporary oppression. Liberals tend to believe that the history of slavery and segregation has lasting impacts that cannot be ignored and must be countered by direct intervention. Conservatives tend to question when we should stop blaming society or a history of oppression, and begin blaming individual choices.

A similar disjuncture applies to the concept of tolerance. Liberals believe that tolerance applies broadly, to all social differences and a diversity of beliefs. Because we have no place making decisions about appropriate belief systems (anti-foundationalism), we must respect the equality of various traditions or choices. Conservatives tend to see tolerance as applying to what you are—immutable or born characteristics—but not necessarily to what you do, or choices for which one can be held accountable. All actions are not something we have to, or should, tolerate. Nor should we be tolerant of all beliefs or ideas, given that ideas have consequences. Perhaps most importantly, we should not be tolerant of intolerant groups. We only embrace those who support the constitutional order, but to enemies of our own foundational system we should not offer the same kind of acceptance. This difference is explained by the distinct liberal and conservative premises regarding social fragility. In the conservative view, we cannot afford to be tolerant of those who would destroy us. It surprises conservatives that liberals support tolerance toward Islamist extremists, or supporters of radical theocratic Islam, because the last thing liberals should be tolerant of is beliefs and people who are adamantly opposed to liberalism, tolerance, or women's rights. The explanation for this is that liberals simply do not believe that the intolerant forces of radical Islam can win or that they are a real threat. Conservatives do.

When we discuss how tolerant we are in America, or how racist, or how much liberty we have, or how much economic opportunity, it is important to be clear about what comparison we have in mind. This reveals another important difference in liberal and conservative thinking, as well as a major source of misunderstanding of each other's positions. Conservatives tend to compare American conditions to the situation in other countries, which makes us look very tolerant, very free, and with a great deal of opportunity for advancement. Another comparison favored by conservatives is to conditions in the past, which creates the same conclusion. On the other hand, liberals tend to make comparisons to a more ideal state of what could be or should be achieved. The appropriate standard is our public ideals, not conditions in other places. With this difference in mind, we can see why liberal claims that we are not tolerant sound nonsensical to conservatives, who wonder why liberals do not criticize other nations even more strongly, which they do not seem to do. It is easy for conservatives to think that liberals are simply uninformed or foolish, as they don't seem to know what it is like in other places or to appreciate what we have here. To liberals, the observation that we are better than other places holds little weight when we are still not what we should be. So we are more free than China, and have more economic opportunity for the poor to advance than Mexico. Congratulations. Let's talk about what we *should* be.

These clashes of perception and definition—of the meaning of liberty and equality, of the basic unit of society, of the nature of government action, of the meaning of oppression and tolerance, and of the proper comparison for our current conditions—drive the policy positions of conservatives and liberals along with the underlying premises and values of each ideology. Their divergent issue stances are the *result* of ideology rather than the *cause* of it. We often hear liberalism and conservatism summarized as a collection of left/right issue positions, but that is misleading. Nonetheless it is important to see what this perspective has to offer. Figure 13.1 shows a standard representation of two dimensions of conservative–liberal policy views. The first dimension is *government intervention in the economy*, regarding regulation of business, spending on welfare programs or unemployment benefits, and environmental controls. The second dimension is intervention in

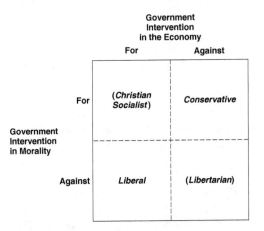

Figure 13.1 Economic and Social Ideology

morality, such as abortion or same-sex marriage. Liberals and conservatives take opposing positions on the two types of government action. This creates a four-square of liberal views, conservative views, and two other possibilities, as illustrated in Figure 13.1.

In the post-9/11 world, foreign policy questions of war and our response to terrorism add a third dimension. This is harder to draw or conceptualize, and creates several different boxes that are no longer simply liberal or conservative, but instead represent subsets within the ideologies. The four-square way of understanding American ideology is not *wrong*, but it simply doesn't explain much. It is a solid description of conservatives as generally favoring government intervention in morality but opposing intervention in the economy, and liberals taking the opposite positions. But it does not explain *why*—or how these positions fit together. It also gives the impression that the policy positions on economics and society come first, and determine the ideology, when it is really the opposite.

The figure does provide insight into other possible ideological positions, some of which are prevalent in America and some not so much. The square in the upper left is hard to define in America, but is a larger player in European politics, where they are known as Christian Socialists, or religious moralists who believe in intervention in the economy to promote goals of social justice. However, the square in the bottom right is an important force in American ideology. While liberals and conservatives favor some government intervention but oppose other kinds, in a way that initially may not make sense, libertarians simply oppose *all* government intervention, which is perfectly clear across the board.

A Note on Libertarianism

This alternative ideology is worth discussing, because it forms a separate perspective that is influential in our politics even while off the usual grid of conservative–liberal competition. Libertarianism is not a constellation of premises and values but instead one single dimension, a commitment to individual liberty. Unlike the other ideologies that require several things to understand their inner workings, libertarianism is much easier to comprehend, grounded in the single principle that individuals should be left alone from government. Libertarians tend to accept that human nature is good, and that society is not fragile. Therefore, one might think they were liberals. But they are not, as they also reject anti-foundationalism, embracing individual liberty as a clear foundation. They value individualism over communitarianism, so therefore one might think they were conservatives. But they are not, as their core value is pure liberty rather than ordered liberty. They have no regard for a golden mean, but lean distinctly to the liberty side, with no fear of anarchy or the dominance of privileged wealth. Libertarians are not impressed with the need for social order, nor impressed with the concern for oppression. Society will take care of itself, and people get what they earn in a market economy. Therefore, both of the central questions and problems of conservatism and liberalism do not resonate with libertarians. They are concerned with freedom, pure and simple.

One way to summarize the libertarian worldview is how it compares to the other ideologies' views of equality and liberty. While conservatism holds to the older view of both values, and liberalism embraces the newer conception, libertarians accept *old equality* with *new liberty*. The Founding vision of equality under law is all the equality humans can achieve given inherent differences in ability and motivation, which should be respected. The earlier vision of liberty, however, is too restrictive, and libertarians desire a more expansive modern vision of individual freedom from restraint.

Another term sometimes used for libertarians is "classical liberals." This is a term for a specific intellectual tradition stretching from Enlightenment figures such as John Locke and Adam Smith up through Friedrich Hayek in the twentieth century, focusing on immutable individual rights and limited government. "Classical liberalism" is easy to confuse with contemporary liberalism, but the two are worlds apart. Unfortunately, the term "liberal" has been applied in very different contexts over the last few hundred years, so the camps are easy to confuse. "Liberal" or "conservative" in one place or time does not mean the same thing as it does in another, which is why this book concentrates solely on contemporary American ideology. No universal definition of the two terms is possible, but only a localized one. The good news is that what matters to us most is how the ideologies are understood within our own politics, and that is clear. What scholars call "classical liberalism" is equivalent to contemporary libertarianism, regardless of the word "liberal" in the phrase.

Because libertarians have a harder time fitting into the current political spectrum, it is important to note how they relate to the branches of the other ideologies. They are not interested in most branches of liberalism dealing with class or environmental oppression, but do resonate with some branches focusing on gay rights and women's rights. They are not interested in social conservatism or national defense conservative, but strongly support economic conservatism. It is common to find citizens who describe themselves as economic conservatives but not any of the other kinds, often even opposing socially or culturally conservative positions. Sometimes they describe themselves as economic conservatives but social liberals. Often these people are not really conservatives at all, nor liberals in any meaningful sense, but instead are libertarians. The usual public discussion of liberal versus conservative simply limits them to the best description they can manage within that limited vocabulary. If we reframed our political party system from scratch, there is strong evidence that libertarians would form a major party, perhaps larger than either clear liberals or clear conservatives.

Libertarians used to identify most frequently with the Republican Party, driven by their agreement with economic conservatives. As our political discussion shifted toward social issues, the libertarian alignment with Republicans became less dominant. Many turned away from the Republican Party because of its religious turn, especially during the George W. Bush administration. Nonetheless, a large group of Republicans are what I describe as weak-willed libertarians, or philosophical libertarians who will grant the need for government action on various issues when pushed. Why are they not strong-willed libertarians? Because taken to the extreme, the philosophy can be criticized easily. Strong-willed libertarians are often accused of being selfish. They tend to be from affluent backgrounds and to be strong market actors who have no trouble being prosperous. They see their endowments as property rather than accidents of luck or chance, and therefore have little sympathy for those born with fewer gifts. They are also accused of being unpatriotic. They tend to have weak national attachments or loyalties, not because they identify with other smaller groups, but because they identify with themselves. But their political positions are easy to understand, because a single principle against government action clarifies their thinking.

Two interesting points about libertarianism are worth noting. The first is that it seems to be rising among young Americans, and therefore may be more influential in the future. The significance of Ron Paul as a national figure is due to the political engagement of many citizens who did not identify with either conservatives or liberals, but recognized a like-minded politician for the first time. The second point is that libertarians are not as aligned with conservatives and sure to vote Republican as before. Economic freedoms used to be the central libertarian concern, in response to increased taxation and the regulatory state. Now the rise of the religious right in Republican politics has alienated many libertarians from the party. Gay marriage as a prominent issue has pushed many young libertarians toward the Democrats. But they are still not truly at home in either ideological or partisan camp.

One way to summarize the libertarian position compared to the other ideologies is to ask what is heroic. What is most respected and admired by each group? For conservatives, it is military warriors, who sacrifice for the group, exhibit strength against a dangerous world, and defend society. For liberals, it is political activists, who improve society by standing up against oppression and taking risks to better the lives of others. For libertarians, it is business people, who build new corporations, structures, and endeavors (what is known as heroic capitalism). What we admire tells us a great deal about a worldview, along with its premises, its values, and its visions of social progress.

14

THE ORIGINS OF
CONTEMPORARY IDEOLOGY

Explaining Neocons Versus Paleocons
and Multiculturalists Versus Liberals

As a final note it is useful to go back to the beginning. Understanding a bit about the origins of contemporary conservatism and liberalism explains a great deal about their differences as well as their internal divisions. Earlier I presented the branches of conservatism and liberalism as offering diverging answers to the distinct questions of each ideology. In our current political conversation there are other important divisions that are worth understanding as well, especially the disagreement between neoconservatism (neocons) and more traditional conservatism (paleocons), and among liberals the division between multiculturalists and traditional liberals.

It will surprise few readers to note that conservatism is older and liberalism is newer. By new, I still mean over a hundred years old. But much newer than American conservatism, which looks to the Founding for its inspiration. One way to understand contemporary conservatism is a high regard for the Founding era and constitutional principle. It is grounded in a reverence for the exceptional American national ideals established at that time. While commentators often compare contemporary conservatism and liberalism to different groups of the Founders—conservatives allegedly descending from Hamilton or Adams and liberals from Jefferson—this is a mischaracterization of the Founders as well as contemporary politics. Most of the Founders held premises of social fragility and negative human nature, and embraced the core value of ordered liberty. They upheld the old rather than new interpretations of liberty and equality described in Chapter 12. Even Jefferson was not a liberal. He might have been closer to contemporary liberals than Hamilton was in some respects, but he was not close at all. This makes perfect sense when we consider that liberalism is a relatively new movement grounded in newer ideas. It simply didn't exist at the time of the Founding, and its originators came later. Conservatism has older origins, but was eclipsed in our national politics by the rise of liberalism following the Civil War, originating in the utopian social movements of the late 1800s. From these origins, liberalism grew in prominence through the Progressive Era, the New Deal, and the Great Society, as well as the social movements of the 1960s and 1970s. Conservatism as a political force gained strength in reaction to these developments, but did not by any means originate only after the leftward turn of the peace movement, the women's movement, and the sexual revolution. These changes and the conservative reaction against them frame our current ideological spectrum. The story has other more recent turns, including the rise of a new form of liberalism—multiculturalism—and a new branch of conservatism, known appropriately as neoconservatism. The divide between multiculturalists and traditional liberals is discussed much less than its importance would suggest, and the future of the clash between neocons and paleocons is unclear. And so the story continues.

Traditional Liberalism Versus Multiculturalism

The origin of any belief system is almost always a matter of dispute, and one can usually discover older and older precursors without too much digging. Few beliefs spring forward from nothing, but instead evolve from earlier ideas. American liberalism draws on several older traditions, but as far as I can tell the emergence of the political doctrines of contemporary liberalism can be found in the utopian perfectionist movements of the middle and late 1800s. Prior to and following the Civil War, many Americans began to experiment with new ways of perfecting society and individuals. They were inspired by religious devotion and charismatic leaders to attempt the creation of better worlds, grounded in new communal social arrangements. These included the Oneida Community under the leadership of John Humphrey Noyes, the Shakers, the Harrisites, the Mormons, and many other groups. Several things united this set of movements: their commitment to religious utopianism, their creation of close-knit communities, and their experimentation with basic social institutions, especially marriage. The Shakers believed that sexual relations were an unnecessary distraction, which explains why they died out, while the Oneida community believed that traditional marriages were a source of unhappiness. Instead they practiced "complex marriage," meaning that all of the adults in the community were married to all of the others, and could engage in relations with each other after a series of ritualized permissions were obtained. The phrase "free love" was not invented by hippies in the 1960s, but by a religious leader in the 1860s. The same religious and political fervor of that era produced the abolitionist, temperance, and women's movements. Many secular liberals would be

103

Table 14.1 Origins of Liberalism

	Communal Perfectionist Movements[1] (middle to late 1800s)	Wilsonian Idealism (pre & post-WWI)	New Deal (pre & post-WWII, FDR to JFK)	Great Society & Civil Rights (pre & post-Vietnam, LBJ to Carter)	Current (1990+ Clinton to Obama)
Perfectionist	X	X	X	X	X
Religious	X	X			
Militarist		X	X		
Anti-foundationalist					X
Multicultural					X

Note
1 Religious communities of the late 1800s, including the Oneida Community, Amana Society, Shakers, Harrisites, Mormons, etc., which were connected to the political movements for abolition, temperance, and other reformist movements.

surprised that their ideas had an origin in Christian thought, but ideas shift over time, often moving far away from their origins.

Table 14.1 traces the evolution of liberalism from these early social movements to the political eras of the twentieth century, including Wilsonian idealism in the era of World War I, the New Deal of FDR, the Great Society of LBJ, and the current version of liberal ideology.

At the core of the worldview is perfectionism. While other aspects of liberalism rose and fell, this core premise is consistent across each of its evolutions. Liberalism first gained political force in perfectionist social movements grounded in collectivism and a positive view of human nature. As liberalism gained national importance it became more militarist, which characterized the idealistic attempts to remake the international system in the era of World War I, led by President Woodrow Wilson in the early 1900s. The more recent history is a falling away of religion and militarism, and the rise of anti-foundationalism and multiculturalism as defining elements, though the perfectionist core remains.

The things to explain in the evolution of American liberalism are the fall of religious faith; the rise of anti-foundationalism as a new core premise; the rise and fall of militarism; and finally the new role of multiculturalism. Liberalism began as more absolutist, framed by the idea of religious perfectionism. The religious foundations fell away after the early decades of the twentieth century along with the rising influence of Marxist and socialist thought in academic and political circles. One did not have to be a true Marxist to be influenced by the changes that this belief system brought about. It represented a full-throated challenge to religious faith as the basis of social change. It was not only atheistic, but offered the mechanisms of technology, rationalized social control, and ideological fervor as a replacement for faith-based improvement. The rising tide of scientific advancement and the increasing rejection of religion in the university also encouraged the rise of secular perfectionism, which became the dominant form of liberalism by the time of the Great Society. Another change that derived from the university world was the rise of anti-foundationalism, which moved from academia into contemporary liberalism. In many ways this idea is the opposite of the religious commitments of early liberalism. Rather than the surety at the core of the abolitionism movement, the newer academic view was the rejection of absolute beliefs, replaced by great uncertainty about statements of better or worse. This opened the door to tolerance as the new core value along with equality.

Early liberalism was more muscular, more sure of itself, and therefore more willing to employ military force and nationalism as tools to forge a better world. The abolitionists were not shy about the need for drawing blood, nor were the advocates of U.S. intervention into World War I. Their internationalist vision of ending wars and establishing a world governing body in the League of Nations was to be achieved through force as well as persuasion. The event that killed the militarist aspect of American liberalism was the Vietnam War. The war and protest environment of that era eliminated the earlier feeling that military force could accomplish positive ends. Regard for military culture and symbolism evaporated among liberals and became the clear province of conservatives. John F. Kennedy represents the last of the nationalist/militarist liberals, prior to the backlash of the peace movement. His definition of liberalism is cited perhaps more than almost any other:

> If by a Liberal they mean someone who looks ahead and not behind, someone who welcomes new ideas without rigid reactions, someone who cares about the welfare of the people—their health, their housing, their schools, their jobs, their civil rights, and their civil liberties—someone who believes we can break through the stalemate and suspicions that grip us in our policies abroad, if that is what they mean by a Liberal, then I'm proud to say I'm a Liberal.

In the same speech during the presidential campaign of 1960 he said

> More will be needed than goodwill missions or talking back to Soviet politicians or increasing the tempo of the arms race. More will be needed than good intentions, for we know where that

paving leads. In Winston Churchill's words, "We cannot escape our dangers by recoiling from them. We dare not pretend such dangers do not exist."

Militarism is a part of this liberal vision, which makes it somewhat anachronistic. JFK's inaugural address pledged to "pay any price, bear any burden, meet any hardship, support any friend, oppose any foe, in order to assure the survival and the success of liberty." Kennedy warned that "we dare not tempt them with weakness. For only when our arms are sufficient beyond doubt can we be certain beyond doubt that they will never be employed." The freedoms that he pledges to defend "come not from the generosity of the state, but from the hand of God." These statements sound more like a contemporary conservative, and would not have been said by Clinton, Kerry, or Obama.

The decline of the religious and militarist aspects of the ideology led to the rise of pure perfectionism as the core of the doctrine. If the evolution of liberalism had stopped there, contemporary beliefs would be characterized by a core concern for social justice focused on economic opportunity and class relations, as it had during most of the twentieth century. But it did not stop there. While traditional liberalism still holds to the view that wealth and poverty are the basic source of oppression, multiculturalism offered a new perspective that has become highly influential or even dominant in some spheres, causing a rift within liberalism. Multiculturalism represents a shift from class politics to identity politics, from the redistribution of wealth to the recognition of identity groups, or as I phrase it, from the politics of mine to the politics of me. Like anti-foundationalism, it emerged largely from academic culture and language, but was also encouraged by the tremendous demographic changes in the American population, especially the inclusion of women, non-whites, and non-closeted gays in the professional and middle-class population.

Multiculturalism was also encouraged by the decline of Marxism. The new branch of liberalism gained momentum in the 1990s after the collapse of the Soviet Union and death of the respectability of Marxist thought in academia. The falling emphasis on class interests as the central source of oppression opened the door to exclusion as the central focus, applying to race, gender, sexuality, ethnicity, etc. Multiculturalism is connected to the concept of "white privilege," or the replacement of the older idea of class or wealth privilege with the rising argument that one can no longer speak of different groups of whites as being privileged, because they all are over non-whites. This is to say that the *primary* privilege is whiteness, and the *primary* oppression is non-economic.

106

Multiculturalists emphasize a group orientation over an individualist focus, emphasizing the broadest possible inclusion of historically oppressed groups. The basis for social justice is broad-based tolerance. A central concern of this approach is language, or the names, terms, and descriptors we employ. Multiculturalists wish to normalize the presence of previously oppressed or excluded groups. Therefore our language must be inclusive, not making underlying assumptions about what is normal or abnormal. The influence of language is a large part of the multicultural movement. This is the origin of what is often called political correctness, which reduces to showing social disapproval of employing older, less inclusive, or potentially insulting terms, jokes, or forms of language. Phrases that imply social differences or suggest that one identity is less than another are politically incorrect and can bring disapproval from multiculturalists. In day-to-day practice, this means that many attempts at humor grounded in the older American norm of poking fun at social or ethnic differences are considered by many to be no longer funny. Humor is no excuse for exclusion. Another way to describe the ideal is that a citizen should be sensitive and sophisticated enough to make everyone feel included. The problem arises because sensitivity and sophistication are often the opposite of humor, which is also valued in American culture.

One way to illustrate the tension between traditional liberals and multiculturalists is their competing views on the universality of our core values such as liberty and equality. Liberalism in its older versions assumes that all humans are the equal inheritors of liberty. Equality also applies to all humans, who are equally endowed with rights. This means that when political or human rights are violated anywhere in the world it is wrong. We may or may not be able to intervene or have the power to stop these transgressions from occurring, but they are wrong every time, in every place. Multiculturalists take a different view, grounded in the rights of groups to hold their own cultures. Our values of individual liberty and equal treatment are just that, *our* values, and we should not impose them on others, especially by force. So are rights universal or the product of cultural variations that we should respect? Are violations of rights wrong everywhere or just here? This question leads to important conflicts in domestic as well as foreign affairs. It is somewhat more obvious in international relations, where we must decide whether we will make an issue of practices in allied or quasi-allied countries such as Saudi Arabia, where they still stone gay people to death and tremendously limit the freedoms of women. Liberals disagree about whether that is a violation of universal rights or a cultural practice of other people which we have no business criticizing.

The domestic question comes to the fore when immigrants bring to the United States cultural practices that violate our norms. One example is female circumcision or the practice of surgically removing the physical source of sexual response from young girls in order to assure that they will remain faithful within marriage. This is a common practice in some parts of Africa and the Middle East, including Somalia. According to scholars who have studied the Somali community in America, the practice is often still maintained here, justified by the desire to uphold traditions and enable girls to make a good marriage match among Somali males who still expect this to be the case as it is in Somalia. The question facing American liberals is whether this violates standards of individual human dignity or whether it is a cultural practice in which we should not interfere. Perhaps more to the point, is it enough of a violation that we will endorse strong government intervention to stop a practice that will continue otherwise. This example is of course at the far end of the challenges to a multicultural position, and most practices in the American mosaic of cultures will be entirely inoffensive or carry nowhere near this level of objection. But the extreme case illustrates the philosophical dilemma between traditional liberalism and multiculturalism.

As a final note, one way of understanding the distinction is to return to the question discussed in Chapter 11 of the basic unit of society. Figure 11.1 illustrates the conflicting perceptions of the holders of rights, or who has the legitimate ability to exercise control over important decisions. Conservatives tend to believe that society as a whole can exercise some rights that restrict the actions of others, especially when it comes to maintaining a decent social order. Liberals on the other hand tend to assign rights almost solely to individuals, who have the legitimate ability to decide their own path without restriction from the community. Multiculturalists tend toward the position that certain social groups can also have rights. Ethnic communities may have claims to their own practices that the majority culture should not restrict. For example, the claims of certain Native American tribes to recognition and specific tribal rights raise this question of individual versus group rights. The heart of the question is whether we define ourselves primarily in terms of the individual, the group, or the whole society.

Paleocons Versus Neocons

Within conservative ranks there is also a division to be explained. The rise of neoconservatism came to the national stage during the 2000 presidential campaign, but had been brewing for some time. In the Republican nomination contest between John McCain and George W. Bush, the younger Bush represented a distinct change from his father's Republican Party, when George H.W. Bush went from being Ronald Reagan's vice president to president in his own right in 1988. The recurring debates among Republicans about which person, and indirectly which belief system, will represent the party reflect an important point we have yet to highlight: that party and ideology are far from the same thing. They are linked in our politics, but not synonymous. Republicans are not simply conservatives, nor are conservatives simply Republicans. A party is a group of people seeking office together, and finding pragmatic ways to achieve that goal. Ideology is a belief system that may or may not aid that practical end at any given time. Much of the current challenge within Republican ranks is against members of the party who are perceived as not conservative enough by some elements of the party. They are accused by more conservative citizens of being RINOs, which means Republican In Name Only, or not the kind of conservative that they want the party to be. The party brand shifts over time as different ideas gain supporters. The current GOP image altered with the rise of neoconservatism, and is now facing another kind of ideological challenge from a new brand of conservatism that rejects neocon policies.

Conservatism as we know it today had a resurgence after World War II following many decades of liberal dominance of American politics through the Progressive and New Deal eras. The rising conservatism was a response to perceived threat and decline. The external threat was the Cold War, or the immediate and continuing tension with the Soviet Union following the victory in World War II, what JFK described in his famous inaugural address as "a hard and bitter peace." The rising Cold War included the Korean War with the communist government of North Korea backed by China, and then the protracted Vietnam War as we fought internally about whether and how we should attempt to counter Soviet and other communist challenges in territory and ideology. The perceived threat from our own form of government was the rise of the regulatory state and the welfare state, both here and especially abroad among our allies in Europe. The threat of internal decline came from the effects of the sexual revolution, the women's movement, and the various other social changes of the 1960s and 1970s on American campuses and in American homes. Rising crime, drug use, teenage pregnancy, out of wedlock births, and many other concerns drove the rising political force of conservatism, especially into the Reagan era.

Reaganesque Republicans can be characterized as paleocons, though the best exemplar may be Barry Goldwater in his 1964 presidential campaign against Lyndon Johnson. Goldwater believed in responsibility at home and strength abroad. We should focus on free markets and individual accomplishment, which leads to an antagonism to big government in all of its forms, including the welfare state, the over-regulation of businesses, and the imposition of federal power into the realm of state and local government. The government is best which governs least.[1] Goldwater Republicans were also pro-military and anti-communist. We must stand up to the Soviet Union and meet their aggression with stubbornness, but not project force into the affairs of other nations unnecessarily. Paleocons have a strong streak of isolationism in foreign affairs. Their nationalism over internationalism includes a sense of difference from other nations, which suggests that we should leave them alone whenever possible. A strong military is a shield rather than an active sword. On these two counts—small government and isolationist militarism—we can distinguish between paleocons and neocons.

Neoconservatism rose from a particular subset of political thinkers who began as Democrats or mainstream liberals in the 1960s and 1970s. Irving Kristol, a major figure in the movement, once described a neocon as "a liberal who's been mugged by reality." Many were staff or supporters of Henry "Scoop" Jackson, the Democratic senator from Washington State from 1953 to his death in 1983. Jackson was an ardent supporter of the American military, the Vietnam War, and a strong posture toward the Soviet Union or other challenges to democracy around the world. Jackson could be described as a militarist liberal, who not only believed in individual rights but believed that they had to be supported and defended by force in international affairs. This legacy became clear in later neoconservative attitudes toward the Iraq War and replacing Saddam Hussein. The Democrats who became neocons were also disillusioned by the failure of the Great Society to change the conditions of poverty through direct government action. They tired of waiting for the Godot that never came, but did not give up on the idea that government can be a force for good in the nation, just as the United States can be for the rest of the world. Because of these beliefs, they are often described as big government conservatives, as opposed to the older conservative vision of limited government across the board. This is one reason that defining conservatism as fundamentally anti-government is misleading.

A third aspect that separates neocons from traditional conservatives is the larger emphasis on social conservatism and the role of religion. This is connected to the rise of the Christian Right as a powerful force in American politics and especially within the Republican Party. Evangelical Protestants have traditionally avoided politics throughout most of American history, believing that any connection between the government and the church would be to the detriment of religion. But several recent disappointments drove them into the political arena. The first was *Roe v. Wade* in 1973, the case in which the Supreme Court permanently legalized abortion. The second was Ronald Reagan. He ran on a pro-religious and anti-abortion platform in 1980, but failed to push for any of the religious agenda that helped him win office. The third was Monica Lewinsky, or more accurately Bill Clinton and the continuing rise of a secular and permissive public culture. In other words, they were not at all pleased that the phrase "oral sex" became a topic of discussion on the nightly news. Paleocons are also concerned with preserving tradition, but are not motivated as much by religious faith. In keeping with their emphasis on limited national government, they are not as interested in projecting religious values into national policy. Barry Goldwater once famously said, "You don't have to *be* straight to be in the military; you just have to be able to *shoot* straight." This would not have been said by George W. Bush forty years later.

Evangelical faith is also connected to an individualist view of the economy and opposition to redistribution policies, in contrast to Catholic and mainline Protestant tendencies toward social justice concerns. This is justified by an individual accounting system of choice, faith, and redemption, as opposed to more group-oriented traditions. Evangelical Protestants tend to respect the accumulation of wealth as a just achievement and sign of God's grace rather than an indication of corruption or a block to divine affection, as sometimes suggested in Catholicism.

But not all of the founders of neoconservatism came from Evangelical Protestant backgrounds. An important group were Jewish intellectuals, such as Irving Kristol, Norman Podhoretz of *Commentary* magazine, or Paul Wolfowitz and Richard Perle, the architects of the Iraq War. The connection between the two groups is the mutual support of Israel as a staunch ally. A part of Evangelical doctrine is that the Holy Land must be controlled by the Jews before the Second Coming can occur. This leads to religious support for the Jewish State, coupled with the traditional American backing of Israel grounded in cultural connections, mutual support for democracy, and longstanding alliances against Soviet expansion into the Middle East and now against Islamist terrorism. With the threat of communism replaced by the threat of the Islamist movement, often described as fundamentalist or radical Islam, neocons have provided ardent support for the wars in Afghanistan and Iraq as well as efforts to prevent terrorism in America.

One way to understand the neocon/paleocon split it to compare their positions on important values that influence foreign policy and war decisions. This can be conceptualized along two value dimensions, creating four categories similar to the ideology four-square figure described in Chapter 13. Along one dimension is pacifism versus militarism, which separates liberals and conservatives. Another value dimension is isolationism versus interventionism. Americans have traditionally held a strong sense of isolation from the rest of the world. George Washington's Farewell Address warned against what he called "entangling alliances" that would drag us into unfortunate world conflicts that we were wiser to avoid. This advice was heeded for many generations and in part explains our lethargy in entering World War II. But after that war and the rise of our status as a superpower, it became more and more difficult to remain on the sidelines of world affairs. Many citizens now believe that intervention is inevitable, or is morally required when we are the only nation strong enough to do good in the world.

Figure 14.1 illustrates the relative positions of several recent national leaders on these two dimensions. Liberals tend to fall in the pacifist/interventionist category. Their version of intervention is grounded more in negotiation than in the use of force, as in Carter's attempts at Middle East peace accords, and Clinton's engagement in the peace process in several world conflicts. Carter leaned more towards pacifism than Clinton, but they are in the same general category. Conservatives are all in the militarist category, but vary widely on the degree of intervention they feel is appropriate. At the most isolationist end of the spectrum is Ron Paul (truly more libertarian than conservative), followed by Barry Goldwater. One could argue whether Reagan or George H.W. Bush was the more interventionist, but clearly the most interventionist was George W. Bush. Neocons are not only big-government conservatives, but also principled foreign interventionists.

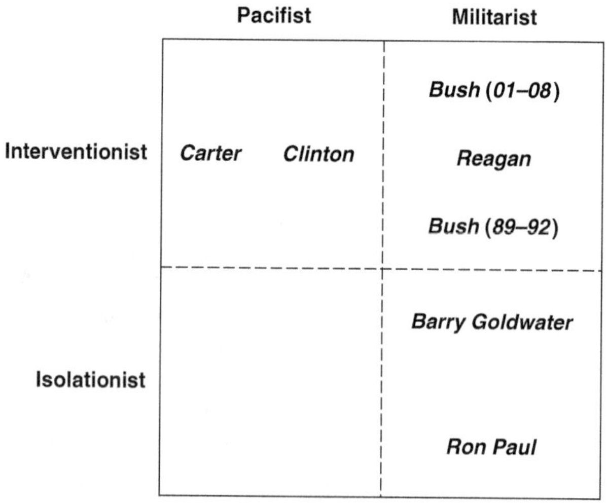

	Pacifist		Militarist
			Bush (01–08)
Interventionist	Carter	Clinton	Reagan
			Bush (89–92)
			Barry Goldwater
Isolationist			
			Ron Paul

Figure 14.1 Military Values and Conservatism

A Note on the Tea Party

Conservatism and the Republican Party are facing a new challenge in ideas and organization from the Tea Party. It began as a grass-roots backlash against neoconservatism among Republicans. Fiscal conservatives and advocates of limited government thought they had an ally in George W. Bush, but what they got was rising deficit spending to finance certain social programs like prescription coverage for Medicare, but especially to finance the wars and the Department of Homeland Security, one of the single largest increases in the federal bureaucracy in the last fifty years. The movement gained strength with the election of Barack Obama and the much larger increases in deficit spending for the economic stimulus, other domestic programs, and the promise of greater costs in the future with the health care reforms. Deficit spending during the Bush administration averaged around $300 or $400 billion after the war spending began in 2003. The deficit for 2009 was $1800 billion ($1.8 trillion), four or five times higher. This spurred the broad anti-spending, anti-tax, limited government animation of the Tea Party protests, which have drawn more people to more public events than any protest movement since the 1960s and 1970s. Political analysts do not know quite what to make of a grass-roots protest movement on the right rather than the left.

The movement played a substantial role in the 2010 Congressional elections that produced a dramatic change in the House of Representatives. Republicans took control of the majority with a gain of over sixty seats, the largest shift since 1948. The first major Tea Party victory was the election of Scott Brown as the new senator from Massachusetts, in the special election to replace Ted Kennedy. Few observers believed a Republican could win a Senate race in such a heavily Democratic state, especially in the seat held by Kennedy for over forty years. In the 2010 primary elections, Tea Party candidates defeated several establishment Republicans to represent the party in senate races in Colorado, Delaware, and Nevada, and ousted incumbent Republican senators to gain the party nomination in Alaska and Utah. Electoral results in the general elections were mixed, and the Tea Party has been credited with creating losses to Democratic opponents by running candidates who were too far to the right or too inexperienced to win. However, major Tea Party candidate victories in 2010 included a new governor (Nikki Haley of South Carolina, the first woman to hold that office) and three new senators (Marco Rubio of Florida, Rand Paul of Kentucky, and Mike Lee of Utah).

The Tea Party movement is not really a third party, and has no recognized central leadership. It may be described more accurately as a social movement grounded in national identification, and a political movement grounded in fiscal conservatism. Tea Party members often employ the term "constitutional conservatism," which connotes limited government along the designs of the Founders, as well as a respect for our long-standing traditions. In the past, third-party movements or sub-branches within a national party have been absorbed quickly into the larger party, which adapted to their demands. Once their ideas are co-opted by the larger group, they tend to fade away quickly. Movements of this nature also tend to coalesce around a specific political leader, such as Teddy Roosevelt with the Bull Moose, or Ross Perot with the Reform Party. The Tea Party has no such central leading figure. This may turn out to be a strength of the movement, which is not dependent on the fortunes of any one leader. As of this writing, the future influence of the Tea Party movement is uncertain.

CONCLUSION

Conservatism, Liberalism, and American Democracy

American conservatism is a worldview that sees ordered liberty as the ideal, or a society in which individual human dignity is valued above other things, such that citizens can live in a free and decent place that is run by neither government tyranny nor public indecency. It is a society of liberty without license. This worldview is grounded in the perceived fragility of our society, the negative quality of human nature, and the futility of utopian fantasies. These desires and fears lead conservatives to embrace the more traditional side of the major value divides in our contemporary culture: individualism over communitarianism; religiosity over secularism; militarism over pacifism; nationalism over internationalism; and the traditional roles of gender, marriage, and children over an openness to new social arrangements. More importantly, the contradictory desires for liberty and fears of social decline lead to the glue problem, or how to maintain a stable and decent society comprised of free individuals who are prone to moral decline. The answers to the glue problem divide conservatism into four major branches: national defense conservatives who believe the best answer is patriotism; social conservatives who believe the answer is God, religion, and moral structure; economic conservatives who believe it is property and free markets; and finally cultural conservatives who emphasize tradition and American nationalism as the glue to a good society. Each of these branches agrees on the foundational conservative premises, the core value of ordered liberty, and the central problem of a decent society, but disagrees on the best approach to reach that goal.

American liberalism is a worldview that sees social justice as the ideal, or a society in which equality among citizens in regard to political power and the ability to lead a good life is valued above other things, such that citizens are relieved from the burdens of oppression that characterize human societies. It is a better world of more enlightened institutions. This

115

worldview is grounded in the perfectibility of humans and society, the inherent goodness of individuals when freed from the oppression of inhuman institutions, and the futility and wrongness of assigning unquestionable truths to diverse people. These premises and values lead liberals to embrace the more progressive side of the major divides in our political culture: communitarianism over individualism; secularism over religiosity; pacifism over militarism; internationalism over nationalism; and an openness to new social arrangements over an insistence on the traditional roles of gender, marriage, and children. The desire for social justice and equality combined with the drive of guilt over past and current ill treatment of other groups lead to the oppression problem, or who deserves our attention and support to alleviate the forces that maintain their unequal status. The answers to the oppression problem divide liberalism into several branches: traditional liberals who see class and economic disadvantage as the primary source of inequality in America; multiculturalist liberals who see white privilege and the oppression of identity groups as the central concern; advocates of race, gender, sexual orientation, or ethnicity as the primary mode of oppression; or environmentalists who see nature as the most oppressed entity in the contemporary world. Each of these branches agrees on the foundational liberal premises, the core value of social justice, and the central problem of alleviating oppression, but disagrees on the best approach to reach that goal.

Perhaps the clearest summary of these competing worldviews is a focus on *protecting versus perfecting* society. Conservatism is grounded in a sense of fragility and a desire for decency amid a world of degradation and decline. The most important thing we can do is protect society from external and internal threat. It is a worldview driven by fear, or to phrase it in the positive sense, love, of what has been lost (nostalgia) and of country (patriotism). Liberalism is grounded in a sense of the possibilities of a better world, even of better people, and a desire for social justice and equality amid a world of oppression. The most important thing we can do is perfect society. It is a worldview driven by guilt, or to phrase it in the positive sense, compassion, for those who do not have the privileges of others.

For readers who have skipped to the conclusion, each part of these descriptions of the two ideologies may not be fully clear, but the preceding chapters help clarify each aspect of the underlying elements that create a cohesive worldview. Each ideology is illustrated through the complete ideology trees shown in Figures 15.1 and 15.2.

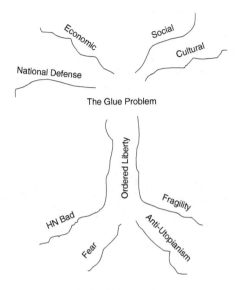

Figure 15.1 Full Conservative Ideology Tree

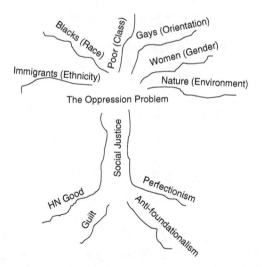

Figure 15.2 Full Liberal Ideology Tree

117

The Poison in the Wound

While these two ideologies can be explained and understood once their underlying beliefs are clear, most Americans, whether apathetic or politically engaged, rarely comprehend both ideologies. Each is complex and counterintuitive. Understanding one makes it more difficult to comprehend the other. But they strongly influence our collective discussions and decisions because our political, academic, and media elites are steeped in ideological thinking. This is not the case with the majority of our citizens, who have strong value systems but not developed ideologies. Many have values that lean to the conservative side, or tend to be more liberal, but not full-blown ideologies. Any given citizen may have parts of the tree, but rarely the whole structure. For some it is a resonance with the core value of social justice or ordered liberty. For others it may be a specific premise like social fragility or perfectionism. The emotions of fear and guilt no doubt motivate many citizens. Or one of the branches of an ideology may reflect someone's life experience. While specific elements of the ideologies drive the politics of many citizens, the whole tree rarely does.

But it is the full-blown worldviews that shape our media conversations and government policies. Once an ideology is in place in our minds, it tells us what to expect before we see it, shapes our observations to fit its dictates, and offers ready-made solutions to problems that are yet to appear. Perhaps more importantly, it creates a disconnect between our citizens and our leaders. Our citizens cannot follow what our ideological leaders are thinking and saying, nor can our leaders understand the more straightforward impulses of a non-ideological public. As illustrated in Figure 15.3, there is not only a gap in understanding between our liberals and conservatives, but also between each group of ideologues and normal citizens.

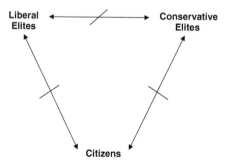

Figure 15.3 Ideological Non-Communication

118

Most Americans do not believe in the elite self-perception of the good ideologue. In their own eyes, ideologues are the champions of a clear-minded vision of what drives the political world and how we should address it, inspired by the belief that their vision is surely correct and their opponents are equally misguided. However, Americans tend to be a pragmatic people who believe more in simpler values and the hopes of honest government. The dilemma created by ideological elites and value-driven citizens is clear, but the poison is in the wound. Nonetheless, if we wish to understand American politics it is crucial to have a working sense of the two competing ideologies. This brief work has succeeded if it adds to that goal.

SUGGESTIONS FOR
FURTHER READING

Conservatism:

Scholars often trace modern conservatism to Edmund Burke, who did not trust people. I trace it more to Thomas Hobbes, who really didn't trust people (see Burke's famous "Speech to the Electors of Bristol" on the role of elites, his *Reflections on the Revolution in France* on the fear of anarchy, and Hobbes' *Leviathan* on the need for order). A Hobbesian world is a basic assumption of conservatism—that without constraining forces, life is "nasty, brutish, and short." While philosophical origins are important, it may be more useful for understanding contemporary ideology to concentrate on more recent commentaries. Some of the most useful are:

- Richard Weaver, *Ideas Have Consequences* (Chicago: University of Chicago Press, 1948). An engaging statement of the foundations of modern conservatism in tradition and authority, this book heavily influenced many thinkers in the post-World War II conservative movement. Weaver argues that societies are indeed fragile and dependent on the beliefs that support them, which is the meaning of the title.
- Friedrich Hayek, *The Road to Serfdom* (Chicago: University of Chicago Press, 1944). One of the most cited arguments for the failure of collectivism, social engineering, and centralized control of the economy. Hayek makes the case that freedom is indivisible, such that loss of liberty in the economic realm inevitably leads to the decline of freedom in social and political realms.
- William F. Buckley, Jr., *God and Man at Yale* (Washington, D.C.: Regnery, 1951). This exposé of liberalism on American college campuses no longer has the shock value it did in the 1950s, but it launched Buckley's career as one of the leaders of the contemporary conservative

movement, which included founding and editing *National Review*, one of the most influential conservative journals. Buckley was also instrumental in the writing of the Sharon Statement, a succinct offering of conservative principles, named for the meeting of young conservatives that took place on Buckley's family estate in Sharon, Connecticut in 1960.

- Russell Kirk, *The Conservative Mind* (Washington, D.C.: Regnery, 1953). A survey of conservative thinkers from many fields, including literature and art as well as politics and philosophy. Kirk emphasizes tradition and religion as the core of conservatism, as opposed to Hayek's focus on economics.

- Barry Goldwater, *Conscience of a Conservative* (Princeton: Princeton University Press 2007 [1960]). This brief work is one of the best single statements in print of conservative principles, written from a paleocon perspective.

- George Nash, *The Conservative Intellectual Movement in America Since 1945* (Wilmington, Del.: Intercollegiate Studies Institute, 1976). Nash argues that conservatism as we know it is a contemporary movement, a reaction against the changes wrought by World War II and it aftermath. His presentation is not about popular beliefs, but about the intellectual leaders of the movement, providing a counterpoint to this volume.

- Irving Kristol, *Neoconservatism: The Autobiography of an Idea* (Chicago: Elephant Paperbacks, 1995). A series of essays on the rise of the neocon movement, by one of its central figures. This collection provides important distinctions from the paleocon views of Barry Goldwater, the economic focus of Hayek, and the traditionalism of Kirk, explaining the neocon synthesis of a more interventionist foreign policy combined with social conservatism.

- Dinesh D'Souza, *Letters to a Young Conservative* (New York: Basic Books, 2002). An engaging format of brief letters explaining facets of conservative thought. It does an admirable job of presenting conservative thinking, with the explicit goal to persuade.

Liberalism:

Many scholars trace the origins of liberalism to Jean-Jacques Rousseau, as opposed to Burke or Hobbes. Rousseau's two best-known statements can be seen as the modern foundations for the liberal premise of a malleable human nature, and for the liberal value of social justice: "Everything is good as it leaves the hands of the Author of things; everything degenerates in the hands of man" (the first line of *Emile*); "Man is born free, but everywhere he is in chains" (the opening line of the *Social Contract*). For more contemporary sources, see:

- John Dewey, *The Public and Its Problems* (Athens: Ohio University Press, 1927). In a series of lectures at Kenyon College, Dewey argued that the public has problems that must be solved, but the greatest of these is the discovery and identification of the public itself, or the recognition of the joint interests among citizens. Nonetheless, Dewey believes that a public intelligence can conquer its problems and improve society through greater deliberation and experimentation, one of the great intellectual statements of contemporary liberal philosophy.
- John Rawls, *A Theory of Justice* (Cambridge, Mass.: Harvard University Press, 1971). Rawls's influential work is considered a major justification of the contemporary welfare state, grounded in his argument that justice is best understood as fairness, which requires that we set up social institutions from behind a "veil of ignorance," or a lack of knowledge of our own position within society. Rawls is not an easy read, nor is Dewey (which has been described as "swimming through oatmeal"). These are academic rather than popular writers, but what they offer is important.
- Barbara Wootton, *Freedom Under Planning* (Chapel Hill: University of North Carolina Press, 1945). Written as a direct response and counterpoint to Hayek's *Road to Serfdom*, Wooton offers an influential defense of "the conscious and deliberate choice of economic priorities by some public authority" (p. 6).
- Calvin Mackenzie and Robert Weisbrot, *The Liberal Hour: Washington and the Politics of Change in the 1960s* (New York: Penguin, 2008). A history of the political leadership of the decade in which "at long last the federal government shattered walls of privilege that white males had long regarded as natural and inevitable. It assumed new responsibilities for the poor, the elderly, the environment, the economy, even the arts and media. It enlarged the rights to individual expression and political participation on a scale that had seemed improbable just a few years earlier. It subsidized health care, funded improvements in education from kindergarten through college, and strove to revive and reshape the cities" (p. 3). This is an excellent history of liberalism as a mainstream ideology at its most optimistic time, before the backlash to its policies and the challenge from the re-emerging right.
- George Lakoff, *Whose Freedom?* (New York: Farrar, Straus, and Giroux, 2006). Lakoff is an influential academic linguist who turned to

SUGGESTIONS FOR FURTHER READING

political writing during the George W. Bush administration. This particular volume is noteworthy for its redefinition of liberty as equality, emphasizing the rhetorical aspects of the liberal position (see Chapter 12 on conflicting definitions of core concepts).

- Paul Krugman, *Conscience of a Liberal* (New York: W.W. Norton, 2009).
- Eric Alterman, *Why We're Liberals: A Handbook for Restoring America's Most Important Ideals* (New York: Viking, 2008).
- Alan Wolfe, *The Future of Liberalism* (New York: Random House, 2010). These last three books are recent partisan offerings defending liberalism while often attacking conservatism. Paul Krugman, one of the most well-known liberal commentators, focuses on the economic aspects of public policy, and offers a partisan interpretation of the meaning of the 2006 and 2008 elections, along with an inaccurate prediction of the 2010 midterms. Both Krugman and Alterman argue that the liberal vision is actually the mainstream American one. In their attempt to portray the ideological as the normal, I believe their historical descriptions are incorrect, but they offer an important window into contemporary partisan debate. To be clear, their implication that contemporary conservatism would not exist without the machinations of a small number of wealthy people who have manipulated our institutions and citizens cannot be taken seriously, any more than the argument that contemporary liberalism was the result of a communist infiltration or a few influential radicals. The two ideologies are the real beliefs of real people, who are worth understanding on their own terms rather than dismissing.
- Wolfe presents the liberal vision as a goal to be achieved rather than arguing that Americans already share it. He also offers a broad sweep of the intellectual history of the ideology, connecting contemporary liberalism to it origins in classical liberalism, but providing a more nuanced discussion of their connection. The first two books, and to a lesser extent the third, employ a specific dodge that should be called out. They focus their description of contemporary liberalism on its origins in Enlightenment liberalism and the individual rights philosophy of John Locke. In other words, all of us are liberals, which is the natural ideology of Americans. This argument builds on what historians call the consensus school of American history (represented by Richard Hofstadter, *The American Political Tradition* [1948] and Louis Hartz, *The Liberal Tradition in America* [1955]), which argued that our shared traditions come from this lineage. While this school of thought makes important observations, current partisans employ it to conflate together

philosophical or classical liberalism with contemporary liberalism. The first is a foundation of Western intellectual traditions, from which both conservatism and liberalism draw ideas, and the second is what current American liberals believe. One is about intellectual history and the other is about contemporary beliefs. They are not at all the same thing. Classical liberalism is a *part* of contemporary American liberalism (as it is a part of contemporary American conservatism), but other important elements also define contemporary liberalism. If it were the case that Americans were naturally and predominantly liberals, we would not have our current ideological divisions, and a book like this one, attempting to explain the two worldviews, would be unnecessary.

One of the best ways to understand the two ideologies is to read the great political speeches of their advocates. Limiting the list to four for conservatism and then four for liberalism, perhaps the most famous as well as the most ideologically revealing speeches are:[1]

- Barry Goldwater, "Acceptance Speech for the Republican Presidential Nomination," (1964): "Extremism in the defense of liberty is no vice. Moderation in the pursuit of justice is no virtue."
- Ronald Reagan, "A Time for Choosing" (1964): "This idea that government is beholden to the people, that it has no other source of power except the sovereign people, is still the newest and the most unique idea in all the long history of man's relation to man. This is the issue of this election: whether we believe in our capacity for self-government or whether we abandon the American Revolution and confess that a little intellectual elite in a far-distant capital can plan our lives for us better than we can plan them ourselves." "Our natural, unalienable rights are now considered to be a dispensation from government, and freedom has never been so fragile, so close to slipping from our grasp as it is at this moment." "You and I know and do not believe that life is so dear and peace so sweet as to be purchased at the price of chains and slavery. . . . We'll preserve for our children this, the last best hope of man on earth, or we'll sentence them to take the last step into a thousand years of darkness."
- Douglas MacArthur, "Duty, Honor, Country" (1962): "The will to win, the sure knowledge that in war there is no substitute for victory; that if you lose, the nation will be destroyed; that the very obsession of your public service must be Duty, Honor, Country." "The soldier, above all other people, prays for peace, for he must suffer and bear the deepest

wounds and scars of war." "I want you to know that when I cross the river, my last conscious thoughts will be of the Corps, and the Corps, and the Corps."

- Ronald Reagan again, "Speech at the Brandenburg Gate" (1987): "Mr. Gorbachev, tear down this wall."
- Franklin D. Roosevelt, "Address to the Commonwealth Club" (1932): "The issue of government has always been whether individual men and women will have to serve some system of government or economics, or whether a system of government and economics exists to serve individual men and women. . . . The final word belongs to no man; yet we can still believe in change and in progress." "New conditions impose new requirements upon government and those who conduct government." "Private economic power is, to enlarge an old phrase, a public trust as well. I hold that continued enjoyment of that power by any individual or group must depend upon the fulfillment of that trust." "Faith in ourselves demands that we recognize the new terms of an old social contract. We must do so lest a rising tide of misery, engendered by our common failure, engulf us all. But failure is not an American habit, and in the strength of great hope we must all shoulder our common load."
- Lyndon Johnson, "The Great Society" (1964): "The Great Society is a place where men are more concerned with the quality of their goals than the quantity of their goods. . . . There are timid souls that say this battle cannot be won, that we are condemned to a soulless wealth. I do not agree. We have the power to shape the civilization that we want."
- Barbara Jordan, "Who Then Will Speak for the Common Good" (1976): "We are a people in search of our future. We are a people in search of a national community. We are a people trying not only to solve the problems of the present—unemployment, inflation—but we are attempting on a larger scale to fulfill the promise of America. We are attempting to fulfill our national purpose, to create and sustain a society in which all of us are equal."
- Mario Cuomo, "A Tale of Two Cities" (1984): "We believe in only the government we need, but we insist on all the government we need . . . We believe in a government strong enough to use words like "love" and "compassion" and smart enough to convert our noblest aspirations into practical realities. . . . And I ask you now, for the good of all of us, for the love of this great nation, for the family of America, for the love of God, please make this nation remember how futures are built."

125

NOTES

1 An Ideology Tree

1 Philip Converse, "The Nature of Belief Systems in Mass Publics," in *Ideology and Discontent*, David Apter, ed., (London: Free Press of Glencoe, 1964). When we look at poll data on American ideology, the usual finding is that citizens identify themselves in proportions of roughly 20/30/50 of liberals, conservatives, and neither one (either moderate or don't know). An important observation is that more Americans identify as conservative than liberal, but perhaps a more interesting observation is that large numbers refuse to identify either way. And very few are willing to categorize themselves at the ideological extremes. The options of "extremely liberal" or "extremely conservative" draw only three percent or less for each category, compared to ten to fifteen percent for "slightly liberal," "liberal," slightly conservative," or "conservative." These surveys lead many scholars to conclude that the public is not broadly ideological, even lacking a clear sense of the meaning of the two terms. For poll data on ideology, one of the most trusted sources is the American National Elections Studies (ANES), conducted every two years across a national sample (see http://www.election-studies.org/nesguide/toptable/tab3_1.htm for their results from 1972–2008). The Pew Research Center, another highly regarded source, has the ideological identification as 20/40/40 in their January 2010 survey (http://pewsocialtrends. org/questions/?qid=1756233&pid=56&ccid=56#top).

2 For the contemporary evidence about political knowledge see Michael X. Delli Carpini and Scott Keeter, *What Americans Know About Politics and Why it Matters* (New Haven: Yale University Press, 1996) and for a summary of its impact on democracy, see Jeffrey Friedman, "Public Ignorance and Democratic Theory" *Critical Review* 12,4 (1998): 397–411. Scholarly works on how our democracy functions or fails because of these conditions include Samuel Popkin, *The Reasoning Voter* (Chicago: University of Chicago Press, 1991), John Zaller, *The Nature and Origins of Mass Opinion* (Cambridge: Cambridge University Press, 1992), Arthur Lupia and Mathew McCubbins, *The Democratic Dilemma* (Cambridge: Cambridge University Press, 1998), and Lawrence Jacobs and Robert Shapiro, *Politicians Don't Pander: Political Manipulation and the Loss of Democratic Responsiveness* (Chicago: University of Chicago Press, 2000). For an alternative perspective grounded in

values, see Morgan Marietta, "Value Representation: The Dominance of Ends Over Means in Democratic Politics," *Critical Review* 22, 2 (2010): 311–329.

3   Isaiah Berlin, *The Crooked Timber of Humanity: Chapters in the History of Ideas* (New York: Vintage Books, 1992), 10. For more academic definitions of values, see Milton Rokeach, *The Nature of Human Values* (New York: Free Press, 1973): "an enduring belief that a specific mode of conduct or end-state of existence is personally or socially preferable," or William Jacoby, "Issue Framing and Public Opinion on Government Spending." *American Journal of Political Science* 44, 4 (2000): 750–67: "abstract, general conceptions about the desirable and undesirable end-states of human life."

4   Daniel Bell, *The End of Ideology* (Cambridge: Harvard University Press, 1960), 370.

5   Clifford Geertz, *The Interpretation of Cultures* (New York: Basic Books, 1973), 207.

2 Conservatism: Premise Foundations

1   Carl Schmitt, *The Concept of the Political* (Chicago: University of Chicago Press, 1927). A contemporary voice that reflects this sentiment is conservative radio talk show host Neal Boortz, who phrased it, "No democracy has survived longer than 200 years and the U.S. has exceeded its life expectancy. Many of my callers are concerned that they are witnessing the dissolution of the Republic" (talk at the University of Georgia with Senator Saxby Chambliss [Republican] of Georgia and Ben Nelson [Democrat] of Nebraska, September 2010).

2   In the Kevin Costner version of *Wyatt Earp* (about the shootout at the O.K. Corral but also the famous lawman's perspective on violence), his father, Judge Earp, tells him when he is young and first heading West, "this land is full of people doing wicked things to each other... You know I'm a man that believes in the law. After your family, its about the only thing you've got to believe in. But there are plenty of men who don't care about the law, men who will take part in all kinds of vicousness, and don't care who gets hurt, in fact, the more they get hurt the better. When you find yourself in a fight with such viciousness, hit first if you can, and when you do hit, hit to kill." Westerns are perhaps an innately conservative genre, a commentary on establishing and maintaining civilization through violence. Another classic meditation on the gunfight is Clint Eastwood's *Unforgiven*. Little Bill Daggett (Gene Hackman): "You just shot an unarmed man." William Munny (Eastwood): "Well he should have armed himself." This reflects Eastwood's famous line in *The Good, the Bad, and the Ugly*: "In this world there's two kinds of people, my friend. Those with loaded guns, and those who dig."

3   See Jean-Jacques Rousseau, *Emile, or On Education*, translated by Allan Bloom (New York: Basic Books, 1979 [1762]), *The Social Contract*, translated by Victor Gourevitch (Cambridge: Cambridge University Press, 1997 [1762]), and Thomas Hobbes, *Leviathan* (Oxford: Oxford University Press, 2008 [1651]).

4   Correspondence with Mark Perlman, dated 11 May 1952, archived at Duke University Library. See also Mark Finnane, *John Vincent Barry: A Life* (Sydney: University of New South Wales Press, 2007).

5 Conservatism: Branches

1   Craig Ferguson, *American on Purpose* (New York: Harper Collins, 2009), viii.

6 Liberalism: Premise Foundations

1 Prominent sources of anti-foundationalism include John Rawls, *A Theory of Justice* (Cambridge: Harvard University Press, 1971) and Richard Rorty, *Philosophy and the Mirror of Nature* (Princeton: Princeton University Press, 1979), but the broad influences of the idea have permeated academic language and argument, which shy away from asserting absolute truths or value commitments as the foundations of society.

9 Liberalism: Branches

1 The cost of a year at many good schools is the same as the total annual income of most American families. The median household income in 2009 was $50,300 according to the U.S. Census Bureau. The cost of tuition and housing at the top ten liberal arts colleges that year averaged $50,200, and for the top ten universities $49,300. Even students who receive substantial financial aid, and work during school, face barriers compared to other students. Simply put, students who work in addition to studying are not on the same playing field as students who have their full time available for studying, not even considering the ability to take the unpaid internships and other resume-building activities that open doors to many professions.

2 "Diversity and the Myth of White Privilege," *Wall Street Journal* 22 July 2010.

10 Emotions and Nightmares

1 William Butler Yeats, "The Second Coming" 1919.

2 Chinua Achebe, *Things Fall Apart* (London: William Heinemann, 1958).

3 Colbert's announcement for his March To Keep Fear Alive, 30 October 2010 on the National Mall, http://www.keepfearalive.com.

11 Value Divides

1 James Davison Hunter, *Culture Wars: The Struggle to Define America* (New York: Basic Books, 1991). Another important work on the topic is Mark Brewer and Jeffrey Stonecash, *Split: Class and Cultural Divides in American Politics* (Washington, D.C.: CQ Press, 2006).

14 The Origins of Contemporary Ideology: Explaining Neocons Versus Paleocons and Multiculturalists Versus Liberals

1 This aphorism is attributed to several different thinkers, including Thomas Paine and Thomas Jefferson, among others. I do not know who said it first, though I know it has been repeated often.

Suggestions for Further Reading

1 Each of these speeches is available in Stephen Lucas and Martin Medhurst, *Words of a Century: The Top 100 American Speeches 1900–1999* (New York: Oxford University Press, 2009).

INDEX

CPSIA information can be obtained
at www.ICGtesting.com
Printed in the USA
LVHW081749060220
646086LV00012B/1106

9 780415 899000